And This Is Why

We Homeschool

By Garrett Ashley Mullet

Special Thanks To:

Lauren, my wife, for supporting my effort to write this book, as well as all the years of blogging and podcasting; she does a tremendous, dedicated, and brave job homeschooling our children, and I am madly in love with her;

My children – Josiah David, Elihu James, Solomon Emmanuel, Daniel Joseph, Evelyn Grace, Enoch Theophilus, and John Lazarus – for being so bright, inquisitive, creative, funny, and inspiring to me; being their father has grown and refined me, and it is a great privilege to call them my children;

My mother, for homeschooling me, and ensuring my brother and I visited as many zoos, museums, state and national parks, and historical places as we could growing up, in order to ground to reality in our minds what we might otherwise have only read about;

My father, for ever being a staunch and relentless champion of the true and the good, whatever the opposition or criticism to such aims and efforts.

Micah, my cousin, for collaborating on writing projects, including this one, for many years now, and for providing a trustworthy and principled sounding board as I arrange my thoughts;

The dozen and a half other folks I sent the manuscript for this book to in the thick of the 2020 Holiday season, who gave me feedback on this work despite my having dropped it on them last-minute.

Introduction

You have just picked up a book on homeschooling.

So now what? You are probably wondering who I am, where I came from, and why I am writing this book. Once we establish all that, you may wonder what you are to do with that knowledge.

And we will get to that, but first things first. Allow me to introduce myself.

My name is Garrett Ashley Mullet. I am a native of Glendive, Montana. I have lived about half my life to this point in my home state, and the other half in and around Hillsboro, Ohio. Now I and my wife and our seven children – six boys and one girl – live in Greeley, Colorado.

As I began outlining this book, I had just celebrated my 33rd birthday. When I finished the work a year later, I was just a little past 34. People tell me I am still "young." So where do I get the temerity to write and speak authoritatively on this subject and expect you to read and listen?

In answer to that, I have been reading up on, writing about, and contemplating social and political issues in America for my entire adult life to this point. And this is what I have observed thus far: so much of what ails or soothes us concerns how we and others were educated as children.

"Train up a child in the way that he should go, and when he is older, he will not depart from it."

So says the good book. This is unfortunately true also in the reverse regarding those children who were trained up in the way they should not go.

To put it another way, if you and I are concerned about the nature of society and where it seems to be headed, we should look to how the majority of those members who make up society were originally educated to give us some idea of where things went wrong.

There is a tremendous ambivalence, even hostility, toward free speech on American university campuses, for instance. Where did that come from?

Who was teaching these students from little on up that they should brook no disagreement on political issues?

The answer for the majority of Americans, and therefore the majority of these students, is the American public schools.

For another example, consider the oft-repeated analysis of the millennial generation, and others. This generation – to which I and my wife belong, I might add – is often characterized as lazy, tech-savvy, entitled, opinionated, narcissistic, frivolous, and self-indulgent.

Now put aside for a moment that seemingly every older generation criticizes the generation that follows it.

Whether those attributions are fair or not, it is fair to ask for good or for ill who brought up the millennials. Who taught them to be the way they are, and who was responsible for their education?

In my case, at least, the answer is mostly my parents. I was homeschooled the latter half of my kindergarten year, the latter half of my 1st grade year, and then every year thereafter until my senior year of high school.

My wife went to public schools from kindergarten through 12th grade.

As we had children, and especially as those children came of age to start their formal education, we discussed what we liked and disliked about how we had been brought up and educated. What had worked, and what had not?

And were there certain things we either did or did not routinely do that were a product of how we were schooled? Were there certain attitudes and presumptions we could trace back to our school days? Were their painful or awkward experiences we would have just as soon avoided, or that we wish our educators and parents would have helped us better navigate? If so, all of that was to be fodder for how we came to a decision on educating our own children.

This book, then, is the product of having been homeschooled myself, talking at length with my wife concerning her public education, and my wife and I together thinking through the decision of whether and how to homeschool our seven children.

This book is also borne out of more news articles and discussions with friends and family over the years than I can count in which, at some point or another, I have commented

"#AndThisIsWhyWeHomeschool."

I know that some people will find this book offensive for its conclusions however carefully I write it and will not be persuaded no matter how strong my arguments or evidence. And those people can criticize and dismiss and be offended all they like, as is doubtless their prerogative. We know the truth is not a matter of counting noses, nor of ensuring no one's feathers get ruffled.

My hope for you, however, is that you find encouragement – literally taking courage – in reading this book. I hope also that you are challenged to think honestly, deeply, and according to wisdom and virtue where our children's educations are concerned.

Perhaps you have already grappled with these questions and come up with different answers.

Perhaps you still have only a vague unease and awareness that greater attention and responsiveness is needed, but you have yet to really start down that path.

Or maybe someone has handed this book to you out of the blue, and all of this is taking you by surprise, catching you flat-footed as it were.

I cannot say where you are at, or what you will ultimately decide to do with your household. All I can do is present the reality of the situation as I know it to be, and trust that those with open minds and sincere hearts will benefit from the exposure.

And this is why we homeschool.

Section I – Parents and Children

Section II – American Public Education

Section III – Homeschooling

Many parents are convinced they could not teach their own children at home. They are wrong.

Homeschooling is not a one-size-fits-all option. That is precisely why you should homeschool.

If you are afraid your kids would drive you insane if they were home all day, here is your sign.

Homeschooling is easier than it looks. But does it have to be easy to be worth it?

Section IV – Opposition

Section I

Parents and Children

Chapter 1

It Takes a Village

You have heard the African proverb, "It takes a village to raise a child." Well, it actually does not. It takes a mother and father.

That said, I will concede the utility of a supportive village. One is nice to have if handy. Whether you are the parents or the child, a community committed to your safety, well-being, and support is a major asset.

This is what scares people away from homeschooling. Yes, there are ugly, unpleasant, frightening, and frustrating things going on in American public schools. Everyone knows this. There is no denying it.

But parents fear homeschooling would mean forgoing community support. And does the good of community support outweigh the bad of all the junk, and all the baggage that comes with the public schools? Most parents are afraid to take the risk of possibly going it alone.

I am assuming you are not currently homeschooling your children. But if you are, you have already been persuaded. And while I may add to your confidence, my guess is that the primary audience for this book is parents who remain undecided and conflicted.

So here you are, presumed audience. You are considering homeschooling, trying to decide what to make of it. And you keep coming back to questions of community. If you are concerned that your child would not be "socialized" enough outside of public schools, you are probably not just concerned for your child. You are probably thinking also of your child's parents.

So, what about you? What about your social life?

The decision to homeschool is a statement. It is a miniature Declaration of Independence. To pull your child out of a public school and teach them at home, you are saying that you do not need, and will not depend on, but would rather be independent from the public education system.

And how did America's Declaration of Independence from the British go? Yes, the colonies won their independence. But there was definitely conflict in the interim. There were hard feelings between Loyalists and Revolutionaries. The British felt betrayed, and thought of the Colonials as ungrateful, faithless, and stupid to want to form their own separate country. Yet in hindsight we Americans almost two-and-a-half centuries later are – many of us, anyway, at least historically – grateful for independence.

And we would do well to consider whether our children will thank us in the decades to come for the choices we make now regarding their education.

Yet that brings us to an important question. When it comes to making these choices, how much do we defer to the collective wisdom of the community around us? How much do we depend on broader society to tell us what is acceptable or not, what is possible or not, and what is beneficial or not?

Research has demonstrated what by common sense we probably should have guessed anyway. Strong psychological pressure to conform is experienced by most people when they observe the majority around them doing something other than what they themselves are doing.

A short video played in General Psychology at Cedarville University back in 2006 proved this point to me.

Hidden cameras recorded the reactions of subject persons unaware they were being filmed as they stepped onto elevators with people already in them.

The people already in the elevators were actors participating in the study, and they were all facing away from the door of the elevator.

When the unassuming subjects stepped on, their discomfort was obvious as they first faced the elevator door. They looked over their shoulder at the other occupants, then looked back again at the door. Squirming for a few uneasy seconds, one by one the subjects of the study eventually turned to facing the same direction as the other occupants of the elevator. They put their backs to the door with no better reason than that everyone else around them was doing that.

We are all susceptible to this to varying degrees and at different times. It is perfectly natural.

Yet it is critical that we recognize in our own personal psychology the tendency to want to go with the crowd against our better judgment.

What if the crowd is wrong? And what if everyone else in the crowd is going along for the same reason you are?

Everyone is assuming that everyone else has done the necessary thinking about whether the present course is a good idea.

If the thing everyone else is doing is not a good idea and you do it anyway, you are sunk unless or until you can somehow break out of the groupthink to reassess your options on their own merits.

This is admittedly an uncomfortable thing to do. Yet if we think about it, the community around us is better for us each doing it when we need to.

Now is as good a time as any to point out something about the argument that we should send our children to public schools so they will experience "the real world."

Has it occurred to us to consider what goes into making "the real world" anyway?

The fact of the matter is that we make the real world what it is by our individual and collective choices. And to say that we make the real world what it is by our collective choices is really just another way of saying that all our individual choice-making comes together to form what we think of as our collective choices.

This ultimately becomes what we refer to with shorthand terms like culture and society.

But to say that we should just accept the way "the real world" is, however it is, without taking an active role in evaluating for ourselves whether that is a good, wise, or useful thing – this is just another way of saying we should be passive rather than active agents in this world.

Should we forgo all moral, ethical, or even practical responsibility for our lives and the lives of those under our watch in favor of doing whatever seems most convenient and easiest at the moment?

Should we each do whatever is right in our own eyes, irrespective of objective truth and morality or the long-term well-being and dignity of ourselves or others?

Should we all just blindly trust that following the herd will take us where we want to go, despite ample evidence that the herd is often as not itself an irrational creature?

When I put it like that, it sounds terrible.

Well that quite simply is because it is terrible.

Horror Vacui

"Nature abhors a vacuum" is a postulate of physics attributed to the ancient Greek philosopher Aristotle. Put simply, it means that if you remove one substance from a container or space, some other substance will invariably rush in to replace it.

I could elaborate what this means about secular versus religious values, or what will happen if we fail to teach our children what they need to know. There are many ways this principle could be applied to the topic of childhood education. But I am instead going to use the principle to express sympathy for those who fear losing the security – or sometimes more accurately the false sense of security – which comes with going along with the crowd.

In other words, it is perfectly understandable that mothers and fathers across America would wonder to themselves as they consider their child's education what will fill the vacuum left by their family's public-school associates. If they suddenly withdraw from the public schools and homeschool instead, nature abhors a vacuum. And nobody wants to be lonely and isolated.

We humans were designed and created for relationship with God and one another. This is at least part of why we recoil at choices which might jeopardize what we perceive rightly or wrongly to be the basis for many of our relationships. This is also why culture can be so hard to change.

That said, do not content yourself with any allusions that there is no solution to the stated problem. Address the elephant in the room. Ask this question and then seek the answer to it. What can fill the vacuum created by a family withdrawing their child from public school to homeschool them?

This can be a difficult question to answer broadly. Everyone's situation is different enough.

Some may have grandparents, parents, siblings, or cousins, aunts, and uncles who would be supportive of such a move. Other extended families may be hostile, but friends are otherwise disposed toward the idea.

Some might have a local church in their community which would stand with them in such a case. Others might find that they receive as much judgment and ridicule from professing believers and even clergy as from the wider secular world around them.

Whatever place you specifically might be able to look to for a greater sense of community, you are not a weak fool for considering the ramifications. It is always wise to count the costs along with the benefits.

Weigh the two categories of things relative one another. There are practical concerns to think about. And these practical concerns for better or worse can directly impact not only your child's health and well-being, but yours also.

Yet it is worth pointing out about whatever community you seek to surround yourself with that you and your spouse and your child would be better off to invest yourselves in relationships which would appreciate and approve of you doing by God's grace what is objectively best for your child and family.

To put it another way, there are many places to look for and build community. But if the place you have been looking would disown and abuse you if you did what you honestly believe is in your child's best interest, perhaps you need a better community.

This is a daunting challenge. I recognize that we all have our limitations.

Sometimes those who love us the most are the most outspoken when we are doing something they genuinely believe will cause us harm. And in that sense, those who criticize you for homeschooling your child if you feel that is the most responsible choice can be forgiven somewhat if and where they genuinely believe – rightly or wrongly – that the risks of homeschooling to your family's well-being outweigh the rewards.

Yet even here, at the end of the day the final decision is ours as parents to do what we believe is best for our children.

And if others are not fully persuaded, but we have diligently done our homework and are persuaded, we can try to bring everyone else alongside.

Or we can nevertheless persevere in doing what we believe is right over and against their objections.

After all, it does not take a village to raise a child. It takes a mom and dad.

And this is why we homeschool.

Chapter 2

Wards of the State

It may surprise you to find out I have friends and family who are public school teachers. I hope not, It really should not. But it may all the same.

Unfortunately, in this highly polarized political climate we have been living in the past few years, people cannot seem to merely disagree with each another. They all too often instead feel the need to demonize those they disagree with and disassociate completely from them.

I recognize that in writing this book, such may well be my fate. Here I am questioning certain sacred assumptions and challenging other norms and trends. Not a few will be tempted to castigate, vilify, and mock me for it.

Yet if that is the price I have to pay, so be it. The stakes of doing and saying nothing are too high. The rewards for trying and succeeding even partially are too great. Therefore, I cannot be silent. And I will not be silent.

Actually, to shock you still further, I will confess that part of what has persuaded me that homeschooling rather than public schooling is the way to go is the common theme I have heard in candid conversations with all the public-school teachers I have known over the years. That is, my friends and family who are public school teachers have confided in me their frustrations. And there is too much in common with their separate complaints for me to dismiss this point as coincidental.

Chief among these, I am told that too many parents expect the public schools to raise their children. Instead of the mother and father taking responsibility to instill discipline in their sons and daughters, they feel entitled to take a rather hands-off approach. Then they blame teachers, administrators, and the system when their children fail to learn much more than how to misbehave.

Similarly, I hear that a lot of public-school children are sent to school without food. The parental presumption here is that the schools will feed the children. And wouldn't you know it? Many schools do! What else are they to do?

But this is a chicken and egg dilemma. So, which comes first? Do parents take responsibility for their own children? Or do the schools discontinue enabling irresponsible and negligent parents?

Yet there is more than that in the mix here. And this is all too often missed when parents and public schoolteachers argue over why the children in America's public schools are not making the grade. The central question here is how much parents should rely on the government to take care of their children.

Another closely related question which we shall get into later is who is ultimately responsible for your child's education. But let us take these things one at a time, shall we?

When we consider the question at hand – that of how much you should depend on the government to care for your child – how should we think of it?

Is the answer all-or-nothing? I think not.

But is the truth squarely in the middle? If you are asking me, that prospective answer is just as ridiculous, and there is nothing whatsoever to recommend it.

Something the famed author C.S. Lewis once wrote in Mere Christianity comes to mind here to characterize both of these two options – the either/or and the middle road. They have "every amiable quality except that of being useful."

But then what is a better way to answer?

In truth, here is where I admit without embarrassment or reservation a bias which is inherent to my political philosophy and worldview. My answer to the central question of this chapter is the same as my answer to the question of how much we should rely on the government for anything else.

In all of the above, I say: As little as possible.

And that answer makes allowance for emergencies.

Suppose a natural disaster befalls the area I reside in, and a truck, boat, or plane comes to rescue my family and me. Will I refuse to be helped on principle just because the persons driving, and helping come on behalf of the government?

Of course not. That would be foolish and ridiculous unless I for an absolute certainty had the ability to handle the problem on my own.

On the flipside, go ahead and assume me to be an intelligent, educated, and able-bodied man.

I have lots of lucrative employment options, and there is no objective reason for me to turn all of these down. But then someone offers me the chance to stay home and play videogames and collect unemployment and food stamps. So, what do I do?

If I turn down job offers to stay home and play videogames and live off the government, something in both me and the system is very badly broken.

And unused muscles tend to atrophy. Perhaps once upon a time I was a sought-after recruitment prospect.

But if I spend years of my life turning down job offers and living off unemployment and food stamps when I could have been gainfully employed, my employability will surely diminish with the passage of time. And not only will I be less sought after because I lack experience, drive, and ambition. I will also find that my capability to do valuable, lucrative work diminishes as more time passes in which I am sitting on my butt getting paid for doing nothing.

That is to say also that parents who have depended on the government to raise their children more or less for them for generations will, in time, progressively lose both the ability and confidence required to teach and discipline their own kids at home.

Moreover, why should they feel any pressing need to? The task is being done for them better than they themselves feel they are able to do it, and all the more as the requisite emotional, intellectual, and spiritual muscles atrophy due to neglect.

So why should they go upsetting the applecart now, trying to take over something they feel ill-equipped to do anyway?

Here the reasonable person will ask whether sending your children to public schools is really like not working and collecting food stamps and unemployment.

To that I will say that it might be. But either way, and in both cases, we really ought to ask ourselves whether the present extent of our dependence is necessary, and whether it does more help than harm in the long run if we can escape it but choose not to.

Where dependence on the government is not necessary in the one case, yet is indulged in out of laziness or irresponsibility, most of us in polite society immediately recognize that those depending on public benefits are taking advantage in something of an unscrupulous way.

But if you add to the unnecessity of the situation that it is also counterproductive to our individual and collective health, happiness, and prosperity in the long run, we must at some point ask why we continue on in a dependent state.

This is true of unemployment checks, food stamps, and public housing on the one hand. But it holds true for public education also.

Addiction

Now I would remind you that I have the perspective of an outsider here.

Not only are my wife and I homeschooling our children. I too was homeschooled for most of my kindergarten through 12th grade years.

That made clear once more for emphasis, I do not believe in only disagreeing with or judging circumstances, situations, organizations, or persons unless we have experienced everything within them first-hand.

A man falls off a cliff while mountain climbing and breaks his leg, for instance. I do not need to personally do the same in order to determine that I do not want to imitate that man if it can be avoided.

And it could only be taken as a bit of dark humor for anyone to reply to me in this, "Don't knock it 'til you try it."

Just so, I do not need to have either attended public schools or taught in them in order to form judgments and opinions about the broader public education system.

We humans have an uncanny ability to learn from others when we choose to.

And you agree with that, obviously, otherwise you would not be reading my book, knowing as you do that you have not experienced all the same things I have in the same ways I have.

It is not necessary, nor even desirable, for us all to experience all the same things in order to make reasonable assessments and come to objectively good decisions about unpleasant things we see others experience which we do not want to personally experience ourselves.

All of this said, there is one aspect in which it is useful to admit and remember that I have the perspective of an outsider where American public education is concerned. That is, when I am about to say the kinds of critical things concerning public schools which I intend to in this book.

Qualifiers aside, the reliance on American public schools from an outside perspective looks an awful lot like addictive behavior and an abusive relationship to me.

Not ever having taken drugs myself, I nonetheless am persuaded I do not want to. And those I have spoken with who experimented with drugs when they were younger but no longer indulge – I have it on their authority that their lives and the lives of their loved ones were not the better for it in any way which justified their past choices in this regard.

Yet observation and experience have shown me that telling an addicted person that what they are doing is hurting them, their family, and friends and that they should stop while they are under the influence of the drug, and before they themselves want to stop – this is often an exercise in futility.

You may have the right of it citing statistics.

You might be right to point out good reasons they should be concerned about their safety and health if they persist on their current path.

Ultimately, however, they are going to rationalize whatever they want most to do. And until they in some measure want to do something other than what they have been doing, they are not going to.

Insert cliché reference here to the difference between leading horses to water and making them drink.

The same goes for those in abusive relationships. A spouse or significant other is verbally or physically abusive. But you just do not know the abusive person like the friend or family member you are trying to counsel knows them. They are not often like that. They have their reasons. They had a hard life. You do not understand. What would your loved one do without them?

You have the right of it objectively. The relationship is toxic. The spouse, fiancé, or significant other is self-absorbed and abusive. But your friend or family member on the receiving end of the abuse will keep going back for more and enabling the bad behavior so long as they cannot imagine living without that abusive person. And at a certain point, they even become addicted to the abuse itself because it becomes part of their normal, everyday life.

But here again is why we must be careful about becoming excessively dependent.

Excessive dependence on anyone or anything besides God messes with our minds. It clouds our judgment. And if we are not careful in a dependent state, we can easily find ourselves scraping to get by when we might have otherwise set ourselves up to thrive.

'Yes, yes,' many parents will say. 'We see the peer pressure, drugs, bullying, school shootings, sexual deviance, and chaos in the public schools. We see that the academic quality being delivered is not ideal.'

But many of these parents cannot imagine life without public schools because we have for generations been so dependent on them.

In short, we have become addicted, and are now locked into an abusive relationship.

And this is why we homeschool.

Chapter 3

Better a Millstone

For a while, I was keeping them saved in a special folder in my internet browser. An article would come up highlighting the latest craziness, and I promptly put it in the folder. A teacher was caught having sex with a student. Several students ganged up to murder a classmate or bully them to the point of suicide. An out-of-control student violently assaulted their teacher on video, in full view of a whooping and laughing class of fellows celebrating the audacity of it all.

Then I gave up. There were just too many. And what was the point when the headlines were so constant?

If I were saving the links to make the case to someone who was resistant to my criticisms of public schooling, surely the larger point would not be difficult to prove. That larger point is this: something in the formation of character in public schools has gone terribly, horribly wrong.

The proof of the pudding is in the eating, as they say. And all the proof needed to accurately assess this pudding can be found in the anecdotal evidence which routinely finds its way into both word-of-mouth in your community and the headlines from sea to shining sea.

These stories are not incidental. Where childhood education is concerned, forming good character should be the chief aim. No other subject or pursuit is as important to your child's future health, happiness, and ultimate prosperity. Not reading. Not writing. Not math. And not even science.

As Theodore Roosevelt once put it:

"To educate a man in mind and not in morals is to educate a menace to society."

It necessarily follows that we as parents need to carefully consider the formation of our children's character when we decide where they will get their education.

This comes naturally to some extent.

Proud moms and dads bragging about the merits of sports participation beyond just physical fitness know this. Listen to them go on about their children learning the importance of hard work, pulling together with their team to accomplish goals, listening to their coach. All those things pertain to the formation of good character.

Yet some of the articles I saved in that folder on my internet browser had to do with coaches and teachers who had been trying valiantly to instill good character in their charges, but who were promptly thanked for their efforts with lawsuits, picketing, and calls for immediate termination.

When coaches not only can but do lose their jobs for saying a prayer on the football field before a game, what does that teach the students?

What sort of character is being formed in them from such morality plays? If the coach retained his job at the expense of continuing to pray, a lesson is being both taught and learned.

And if the coach lost his job by sticking to his guns – here also, character of one kind or another is formed and reinforced.

So also, teachers have to be careful if they talk about their Christian faith. Otherwise, they quickly find themselves in the sights of ACLU types crying "Separation of Church and State" – a phrase not from the Constitution or Declaration of Independence, by the way. It was originally from one of Thomas Jefferson's private letters.

I personally prefer the more neutral and amiable language from the Bill of Rights – that whole bit about *"Congress shall make no law respecting an establishment of religion or prohibiting the free exercise thereof."*

Those hostiles to Christianity in American public life recognized the truth long ago. Capturing the public schools was the ticket to transforming the wider United States into a far more secular place.

The tragic consequence has been that in the process of stringently secularizing America's public education system, the character formation so critical to healthy childhood development was effectively jettisoned.

As time has gone on, we find that the character of the younger generations of Americans has morphed into something alien and monstrous.

Yet religion was never wholly banished from the public schools. Only a certain religion was. Only Christianity was banished.

And in the place of honor which Christianity formerly occupied, a new civic religion was erected.

In the name of this new civic religion of Progressivism, children are taught every kind of sexual deviance is normal, healthy, and laudable. This is called liberation.

Meanwhile, Communism, Islamic terrorism, and illegal immigration are not all that bad. And they are certainly not evil.

In fact, when effectively challenged or opposed by an ostensibly Christian America, these and other competing elements have been the innocent victims.

Thanks to the pioneering efforts of historical revisionists like Howard Zinn, our children have been taught that conservatives and Christians are on the wrong side of history.

And repeat after the system. Climate change is an imminent and existential threat. We are killing the planet with all our productivity and exercising of the dominion mandate.

The reason for all this is simple.

Education can never truly be neutral where larger questions of worldview, morality, and religion are concerned.

Here again, as with the rest of the universe, we find the principle of horror vacui in full effect.

Nature abhors a vacuum.

Take one thing out of the container or space, and some other thing must rush in. In this case, the Christian worldview was taken out of childhood education. And Progressivism took its place.

These Little Ones

In both Matthew 18:6 and Luke 17:2, Jesus said that:

> *"...Whoever causes one of these little ones who believe in me to sin, it would be better for him to have a great millstone fastened around his neck and to be drowned in the depth of the sea."*

This may sound harsh. And if anyone but Jesus had said it, we would be appalled by the lack of Christian charity. But Jesus said it. And we Christians must believe he meant it.

The focus of Jesus here is not being harsh toward "whoever." Rather, the chief aim of this passage is Jesus announcing God's protectiveness toward children.

But who is Jesus talking about when he refers to "whoever"? There are at least two possibilities:

First, Jesus is referring to people who systematically and intentionally de-convert Christian children and lure them away from the faith.

Second, Jesus is referring to people who gleefully corrupt minors – not only teaching them it is okay to be wicked and sinful, but actively encouraging them to experiment with immorality.

Both of these categories of people we are promised that God will judge harshly apart from repentance and the redeeming work of Christ.

Yet repentance and the redeeming work of Christ will invariably transform those people who relate to children in this way to the point that they turn from such sins.

But if this is the case, then what is God's mind about American public education as it stands today?

You may not believe it is yet time for talk of millstones to enter the conversation.

Yet if not now, what ingredient is missing? If not now, I cannot imagine at what future point we will admit that the American public schools are systematically corrupting the morals of minors.

And suppose we are at that point now. I have to ask as one Christian parent to another. How can any Christian mother and father in good conscience send their children into the public schools?

And remember, this is for posterity. So be honest.

If we read what Jesus said and conclude it could not possibly apply to American public schools, I cannot believe we reached that conclusion after carefully considering the relevant facts of the matter.

And if in America there is some institution for which Christ's millstone line would be a more relevant call to repentance, direct me to it.

All the ingredients are here. America's public schools are systematically opposed to anything overtly Christian – in word, deed, or precept – being displayed positively.

What is more, these same schools across the country actively promote to their charges what God has clearly marked as degeneracy, folly, and vice.

If Jesus would not have threatened these schools with the bit about the millstone, do tell.

But I think the real reason American Christians react against such talk is that it makes them uncomfortable. It drives them to unpleasant conclusions they would rather not face.

And more to the point, they are confronted by decisions they would rather not make.

For instance, does a parent who knows American public schools are discouraging Christian faith and actively promoting wickedness and folly share the blame with those who would corrupt their children when they send those same children to be taught in those schools?

Would Jesus say it was better for those parents also to have a great millstone fastened around their necks?

This is an unhappy thought, so I will change the subject.

Train Up A Child

If good character formation is the chief aim of education, let us turn our attention to how you go about forming good character in children.

Now whether or not you agree that any education can actually be neutral where moral, spiritual, and religious values are concerned, I do not believe this for a moment.

Yet supposing it is possible for the sake of argument, you cannot form good character in children by putting them into even a supposedly neutral environment.

This brings us to a deeper philosophical question which is at the heart of my conviction.

Are most people inherently good?

Is the critical thing where childhood development is concerned merely to not muck it up?

The assumption here is that a child is automatically on the right path from birth. And we as parents are the ones at fault if they go astray.

Someone or something must have led our children down the wrong road if they were inherently good from the start and ended up being not so good in the end.

An alternative theory is that people are not inherently good.

As a Christian, I believe that ever since Adam and Eve took the forbidden fruit in Eden, human beings have been born with a sinful nature.

In this view, children are born on the wrong path rather than the right one. And it actually takes more work to put them on the straight and narrow rather than the broad path.

If we leave our children to their own devices, therefore, they will become spoiled and rotten. And if we give them encouragement in the wrong direction, they will certainly go that way with just a little effort.

But to get children to become virtuous, useful, and honorable – this is a task that requires concentrated effort, energy, and intentionality.

Proverbs 22:6 gives us the following guidance:

"Train up a child in the way he should go; even when he is old he will not depart from it."

It stands to reason in the opposite direction also.

If a child is trained up in the way he should *not* go, even when he is older, he will keep on like that.

And from this, we should consider the way those who are older today carry on. And how were they trained up? Was it in the way they should have gone or not?

And if they were trained up in the way they should not go, who was training them up, and how, and where?

If that fate is not what we want for our children, we must be sober and vigilant.

And it is not a minor point that we ourselves must know the way our children should go.

As C.S. Lewis puts it, we all innately believe in a universal standard of good and evil. If you think otherwise, carry out a simple test.

As soon as you believe yourself wronged by some other person, watch yourself instinctively assume and refer to a universal standard of good and evil as if the other person knew it too, and was just as subject to it as yourself.

You may argue back and forth as to which of you actually transgressed this universal standard, or what the precise details of it are pertaining to your conflict. But you and I and all of us instinctively know it exists.

Yet to go from this general knowledge to a more specific familiarity with 'Natural Law' or God's Law, or whatever you want to call it – this step in the process cannot be skipped.

If we are to determine what way our child should go and not depart from when they are older – and we must do this so we can train them up in it – we must familiarize both ourselves and them with God's Word.

And this is why we homeschool.

Chapter 4

Whose Responsibility Childhood Education Is

If the good Lord wanted our children raised by others, it is odd that he did not have them born to those people. So, my wife and I ruled out daycare and public education early on.

We just could not see the point in having our progeny carted off for someone else to care for most of the day when we were able to do it as well or better ourselves.

But before I expand on that, you can stop me there.

What about working parents?

What about extenuating circumstances?

What if both the husband and wife need to work?

Sometimes it cannot be helped.

Perhaps I am being unfair.

Or perhaps the answer is that one spouse or the other should quit their job so they can stay home.

This answer seems especially intuitive to me because it is precisely what my wife and I did.

And this is what all the other homeschooling families we know have done.

But I will concede that sometimes this is not feasible.

Single-parent homes cannot typically afford this, for instance. Too many children are born out of wedlock, and plenty of American marriages still end in divorce despite a downward trend in this regard. So, what about the children from those homes?

Also, what about when the husband or wife suffers from a major illness, or they die unexpectedly? The remaining parent has no other choice but to work.

If you are in one of those situations, you have my sympathy rather than my condemnation or criticism. I genuinely mean that.

To be clear, this book is not intended to serve as a comprehensive guide for absolutely everyone to navigate absolutely every possible situation. My intention was never to write an all-encompassing encyclopedia of parenting and education.

Rather, the goal is to get at the universal truths and principles of righteousness and wisdom with regards to childhood education, and to in this work unpack those for you to whatever extent God's grace enables me to understand and communicate them clearly.

But perhaps even this seems rather lofty. I anticipate not a few readers scoffing. Here I am placing myself on a pedestal. Here I am handing down divine precepts from on high to you and yours. Just who do I think I am, talking down to you all? Who am I to tell you what you should do with your children?

I do not know everything. Even where what I do know is concerned, I do not always understand the full implications of what I know. Yet I do know and understand that.

Moreover, regardless oft-deceiving appearances, we are all in that same boat in this regard. We all have incomplete data. We are all flawed human beings. That does not stop other people from writing books. And if it does not stop others – all of whom have to be taken with at least some grain of salt – I fail to see why I should not write this book for you, in hopes it helps the lot of us to be better stewards of our children.

No, my family is not perfect. We do not have it all together. My bunch sometimes bickers and complains. Our abode now and then loses its harmony, just like everyone else's.

We are, in a word, human.

Fortunately for the lot of us, knowing and imparting universal truth and goodness hinges not on either me or my family having it all together. On the contrary, it is precisely because we are intimately familiar with our weaknesses that we must all the more be diligent, particularly where ours and our family's spiritual orientation is concerned.

Not all choices we might make are equally virtuous, wise, or expedient. And the last thing I want to suggest to you is some flattering nonsense to the contrary about how it does not matter how you choose to raise or educate your child.

Not all options are equal in their merit or reward! Not all choices are equally valid! Au contraire, there is an undeniable disparity – not only between public, private, and home education generally, but between the many different subroutines one must choose within each of these major kinds of schooling.

But here is the unifying, equalizing truth: whichever of these you as a parent choose for your child, your child's education first and foremost is your responsibility. That is the big idea.

In other words, if you – like most American moms and dads – choose to send your sons and daughters to public schools, your duty to ensure they are forming good character and a good understanding of the essential subjects does not lessen, not even a little.

Adding teachers, principals, and other administrative officials into the mix does not diffuse your obligations. Nor does it water them down. At the end of the day, remember the sign on Harry S. Truman's desk.

The buck stops here.

So, pay attention. Do your research. Think through the ramifications carefully. Be engaged, and only all the more if you have entrusted your children to someone else to teach and to train.

Diffusion of Responsibility

Diffusion of responsibility has fascinated me ever since I took Dr. Firmin's General Psychology course at Cedarville University back in 2006.

For those unfamiliar, the concept is simple. In any group of strangers where no recognized leader or authority figure is present, each individual within the crowd is less likely to recognize an emergency, seize the initiative, intervene, and help. And this becomes increasingly the case the larger the group of strangers gets.

In practical terms, someone out of a group of five strangers on a sidewalk is more likely to help another stranger drowning, choking, having a heart attack or seizure, being attacked by a mugger, or whatever, compared with someone out of a crowd of ten, twenty, fifty people or more.

The reason for this is that each individual in the group looks around at every other person in the group. Every individual stranger in the crowd is waiting for someone else to take the initiative. No one elected you to be the leader. Surely someone else must be in charge here.

But if every stranger in a crowd remains passive in the event of an emergency, the fact of everyone else around each individual doing nothing serves to reinforce the individual and collective passivity and non-intervention. In other words, the passivity of the group becomes a self-feeding sort of paralysis. Non-intervention then serves to reinforce and build on itself, making more secure each individual in the sense that no one else is too worked up about what is going on. So why should they be?

More is in play here than just individuals being shy about assuming a mantle of leadership. There is also the fact that the larger groups get, the less individual responsibility – or rather, blame – any one person will feel in the event of a worst-case scenario.

Suppose there is an emergency, and someone is maimed or killed while the group of onlookers remains passively disengaged. What is $1/5^{th}$ of that guilty feeling? How about $1/10^{th}$, $1/20^{th}$, or $1/50^{th}$?

The smaller the share of guilt each person might feel if the unassisted person is seriously hurt or dies, the less likely it is that any individual will engage in helping behavior.

This is closely related to the earlier thing I wrote about conformity experiments involving elevators. The psychological pressure to conform to what those around us are doing is incredibly strong and can only be overcome with deliberate intentionality.

We need to recognize the numbing effect of non-action and ambivalence on the part of those around us. And we must somehow train ourselves to rise above it in order to see things as they are and respond appropriately.

Part of how we do this is by reprogramming ourselves to assume a default posture of aggression and assertiveness in the most positive sense of those qualities.

When I say this, I do not mean we become hostile or unkind. What I mean is that we proactively attack problems instead of passively waiting for circumstances to change on their own for better or worse.

Despite our best efforts, bad things happen. But when bad things happen, we take responsibility for tackling what can be done to improve the situation and we help the people around us to the best of our abilities.

Now you may be thinking to yourself that this is all interesting. But what does it have to do with homeschooling? Let me explain.

You have heard that it was said that it takes a village to raise a child, but I say unto you that it takes a mother and a father. The problem with parents not being ultimately responsible for their children's education is that it begs the question of who else would be.

If not you as the mother and father, whose job is it to ensure your son and daughter learn what they need to know to live a happy, healthy, holy, and productive life once they reach adulthood?

For the sake of argument, suppose it is the school's job. Which school? You fathers and mothers have to choose one.

Having settled on a school, suppose it is now the job of your child's teacher. But there are so many teachers who each play a supporting role in the course of a typical Kindergarten through 12th grade public education in this country. So, who are your child's teachers?

Two teachers disagree on precisely what is best for your child. And some of your child's teachers are awful, and others are wonderful. As a result, your child will learn to love some subjects and hate others.

This is the problem with saying your child's education is primarily the responsibility of the public school or the teachers within the school. Saying that is too near to saying your child's education is everyone's responsibility.

And the problem with saying that anything is everyone's responsibility is that this means that thing is actually nobody's responsibility.

If your child's education is that thing which is everyone's responsibility and nobody's all at the same time, you may as well admit that your child is on their own. Sink or swim, little Johnny and Suzie.

This is the "real world" most people are talking about, I am afraid. And I feel like I am watching a wildlife documentary sometimes when I hear parents talk about education.

Will the baby wildebeest or water buffalo become food for the lion, leopard, or cheetah, or will he or she make a successful escape this time? In all the wildlife documentaries I have seen, it depends on what the herd does. But more often than not, the herd just runs off and leaves its weakest and slowest members to fend for themselves.

The herd mentality is soon enough just every wild animal trying to save its own skin, making a mad dash to distance itself as quick as possible from the ominous teeth and claws. Despite the proven collective strength of the horns and hooves, and the supposed strength in numbers, the self-preservation instinct typically takes precedence. So, the herd flees rather than standing its ground.

In theory, one would expect all the lions, leopards, and cheetah to go hungry before ever again feeding on a wildebeest or water buffalo which has a herd to call home. And when the wildebeest and water buffalo have the presence of mind to unite against their foes, this is what happens. Those predators go hungry and saunter off.

But more often than not, a defenseless calf is only saved from becoming the big cat's lunch by the protective parental instinct of the mother who charges headlong and quickly to break up the chase.

In any event, we should not be looking to the animal kingdom to learn how to parent and educate our children. Enough of nature's mothers and fathers eat their own young when given half a chance, and we do not want to go imitating that.

Yet if we look to the God in whose image we were created, we find a better example.

I am reminded of John the Baptist. In Luke 1:17, the prophet Malachi is quoted as having prophesied about him:

> *"...And he will go before him in the spirit and power of Elijah, to turn the hearts of the fathers to the children, and the disobedient to the wisdom of the just, to make ready for Yahweh a people prepared."*

We should pray for this kind of revival to sweep our country. And when we speak in generalities about the problem of fatherlessness in America, and how such is a common thread with all school shooters and so many in America's prisons, and so many other social and political ills besides, we should recognize the power for good inherent to God turning the hearts of the fathers to their children.

But it is one thing to agree in general about what other people in the aggregate should do. It is fine to yammer on about how much better such would make the world if everyone else got their act together. We can wax eloquent all we like about trends and culture and broader society. So, wax on. And wax off.

When it comes to our sphere, our household, and our children, what then?

We cannot control what society does. And we cannot single-handedly change culture.

Yet we can, little by little, affect what comes to be known as the "real world" around us when we each individually accept responsibility for how we order our own household, and choose to pursue wisdom and righteousness in the conducting of our own affairs.

In other words, we can make this "real world" everyone is always talking about a better place when we each take personal responsibility for our own children's education.

And this is why we homeschool.

Section II

American Public Education

Chapter 5

Education as Blood Sport

When you hear the phrase "the real world," what comes to mind?

If you are like me, you do not picture Utopia. And if we are playing a word association game, rainbows, unicorns, and free ice cream are probably not your first thoughts either – except on the off-chance you are an 8-year-old girl.

Speaking for myself, I do not assume that "the real world" is a place where you can readily trust every other person you meet. You do not leave your keys in your car and the front door of your house unlocked at night there.

As we who have been around for a while can attest, real life can be rather dog eat dog. Therefore, we take care. We exercise caution. And we look both ways before we cross the street.

In my experience, references to how the "the real world" actually is always serve as a gentle reminder of these facts at best, or they border on outright cynicism at worst. But from best to worst, I have never been lectured by the naïvely optimistic about the facts of life and things being better than I supposed when the phrase "the real world" is cited.

No, it is always the jaded who have been burnt. And here they are to tell me once again I had a rather too rosy view. And I should dial that back.

'Once bitten, twice shy.'

In light of this, what should we make of claims that American public education is what is best for our children because it prepares them for "the real world"?

I understand our children must grow up some day to find the world has its bullies and tyrants. These little ones will soon enough discover a mix of kind and cruel people. Our kids must eventually learn that there is violence and perversion and confusion and chaos out there.

Yet if this is what is alluded to when people say that public school prepares our children for life as it is – that our children should be daily exposed to all these things and more in their adolescence – I say we should not be either so quick to agree, or else avert our eyes in embarrassment at our own over-protectiveness and unreality.

Consider the case of the Columbine school shooting in 1999. However you think that atrocity might have been avoided in hindsight, we all wish it had been.

But suppose we were to find out something similar was about to take place in our local school. Of course, we would do all we could to prevent it.

And supposing we could not wholly prevent it, we at least would do all we could to protect as many children as possible from being harmed.

And supposing our hands were tied when it came to saving any children besides our own, surely we would at least do all in our power to save at least our own children.

Right?

In hindsight regarding any school shooting or teen suicide brought on by bullying, I dare say no parent of a child directly harmed thought of that outcome as "the real world" they wanted their children exposed to when they committed them to the public education system.

Yet this naturally begs the question to my mind. At what point do we draw the line on how "real" we want things to get for our children? If not at the point of school shootings and teen suicides, then at what point prior to those tragedies?

Concerning Presuppositions

Consider the worldview of the public education system. Whatever it may have been in your parents' or grandparents' day, today it is undiluted secular humanism.

Yes, I know there are Christian teachers, coaches, and staff in public schools across the country. And may the Lord guide and protect them. But their worldview has to remain almost entirely private on pain of lawsuits, public ridicule, and contract termination.

In general, children who attend American public schools receive instruction that is man-centered, naturalistic, secular, and amoral apart from utilitarian, humanistic ethics. And this is by design.

Keep Jesus to yourself. Pray quietly in a way that does not bother anyone else. Be careful who sees your Bible. Do not talk about sin and judgment and the need for a Savior. You can believe there is a Creator. But you will be mocked.

The official curriculum must state that we arose by chance. We are all just the products of randomly beneficial mutations over millions and billions of years of unguided evolution. Natural selection chose the fittest specimens to survive and perpetuate their lines. An unfathomable amount of death and dying, of striving to either eat or not get eaten is how we got to where we are today. That is just the way it is. That is how we got here. And that is "the real world."

In short, American public schools instruct our children that "the real world" is a godless one. Why then should not those same children engage in every kind of self-indulgence that suits them, so long as they feel it benefits them and they can get away with it?

"Eat, drink, and be merry, for tomorrow we die."

Of course, children are not told in so many words that they should pick at and prey on one another. But they pick this up as a matter of course if picking and preying on one another happens to be their drug of choice or the best way to survive.

And when instead of being the ones picking on others these children find themselves the ones being picked on, and when there is insufficient conviction and capability and awareness on the part of the authority figures – parents, teachers, school administrators, et cetera – children in American public schools all too often conclude they are on their own. And then they take matters into their own hands.

Sometimes this takes the form of substance abuse. Other times it takes the form of physical violence, whether towards themselves or others.

When this occurs, what is the reaction from the powers that be? They insist on additional funding to hire more teachers, to pay good teachers more, or to develop and expand mental health programs. Or they say social media needs to be monitored more closely for warning signs. Or they propose stiffer restrictions on firearms and other weapons.

Yet the rhetoric on television, in print, and at the podium never seems to address the elephant in the room.

That is, our children are being given over to education as blood sport. They are taught that there is no God, implicitly when not explicitly. We are all products of random chance, here by cosmic accident, except by the ruthlessness and cunning of our ancestors who did bite and claw their way to the top of the survival pyramid.

Since there is no absolute moral authority, only self-indulgence and expedience, there is little to nothing to say these children cannot harm themselves and one another when such seems to them the most desirable option.

If we are all just animals, then why not reach for the nearest gun or knife to get what we want? That, after all, is the modern equivalent of our pre-historic biological ancestors having used their teeth and claws in pursuit of their needs and desires.

But if the answer to the riddle of why we are getting school shootings and bullying and such high rates of teen substance abuse and self-harm is so obvious, why don't the highly educated adults in charge of this system just say so?

The answer to this question is two-fold.

On the one hand, a good many of them much enjoy living in a system where the worldview leaves them free from the constraints of God and Christian morality. They personally prefer not being held accountable to the same by their fellow citizens in whose name they ostensibly serve.

On the other hand, a great many others who know better in American public education are afraid of the firestorm they would bring down on themselves to question or outright challenge or reject the paradigm of modern American public education. Their careers and livelihoods would be over. Their professional relationships with colleagues, students, and the families of students would be irreversibly altered; and their personal relationships with the same likely would be severed entirely.

In other words, not a few teachers greatly enjoy and feel comforted by the godless, amoral nature of American public education. And quite a lot of other teachers are simply afraid to lose their jobs and their ability to influence the people they genuinely love and are concerned for.

To be clear, this is not a book primarily about psychoanalyzing Christian men and women who work as public-school teachers, coaches, and staff. I am not here to say whether they should be doing more or different than they are in any kind of broad-brush characterization of their efforts. At least for the purposes of this book, I will leave that between the good Lord and those men and women.

However, there is something to be said for two facts of the situation which are related to a third condition.

First, the Christian men and women who serve in American public schools are thoroughly muzzled by the system as it currently stands and has stood for some time now. There is no denying this.

Second, these same Christians in the system are looked at and to by parents who keep their children in the public schools as a kind of proof that the system is not all bad.

Now those are the facts. And the condition they produce is one in which a false sense of security and well-being is perpetrated by the illusion that children are receiving a sufficiently godly influence in their upbringing and education by the mere proximity to muzzled Christian adults who cannot overtly instruct them according to the Christian worldview.

This is about as useful as being handed a locked smartphone to use in the event of an emergency while the passcode to get into it is withheld from you.

This is like parking a shiny new car outside someone's house and calling that a gift while withholding the keys from them.

In other words, the dear, sweet men and women of Christian character who are prevented from overtly sharing their Christian worldview with students in the public education system are not so useful to the formation of godly character and the obtaining of a godly education as many Christian parents in America want to tell themselves.

Give me a perfectly good gun to keep in my nightstand but prevent me from owning any ammunition. And suppose someone breaks into my home in the middle of the night. Any false sense of security I might have derived at possessing a gun with no bullets will increase my vulnerability rather than my security. Unless the intruder is frightened by the mere appearance of my firearm, and assuming he does not know I have no bullets, the gun will do me less good than the nearest blunt object.

Just so, a disservice is done to children from Christian homes who are sent into American public schools on the belief that the presence of Christian men and women in the system sanctifies it even as those same Christian adults are not allowed to actually teach a Christian worldview to those children.

And if the truth were told, the children brought up in this environment are being taught many uncomfortable things about "the real world."

For one thing, they are being taught to keep their Christian faith on the down-low if they value their future livelihoods.

For another, they are being shown that America is not to be governed according to Christian principles. If the schoolhouse cannot be, then neither will the legislature, courthouse, or White House.

Christians can perhaps be tolerated as quiet servants, so long as they meekly and obediently stay in line. But the real power must go to godlessness and the godless. They will make the rules and set the agenda. If you want to get anywhere of note in this country, you had better learn to kowtow in a hurry.

This, of course, is not the hallmark of a quality education – or at least not an education Christian parents should want for their children. On the contrary, this is indoctrination in an opposing ideology, plain and simple.

But we are Christians, not secular humanists. Therefore, the best way to prepare our children for "the real world" is to figure out which educational option most accurately conveys to them what is good and true according to God.

And this is why we homeschool.

Chapter 6

Conducive Environments

My mother had a bachelor's degree in piano performance and was working on her master's degree in the same before she married my dad. Growing up, Mom played piano at home throughout the day, and taught piano lessons to children and adults in the community who came over to our house.

When I was in high school – still homeschooled, mind you – she played accompaniment for the choir at the local public high school in town. Sometimes I would go with her to the high school choir practices and turn pages for her as she played.

I will never forget one afternoon when we pulled up to the school, and there were several patrol vehicles for the local police department parked outside.

As we learned, the police were at the school for a random search, going down the hallways with drug-sniffing dogs to check lockers for contraband. The school was on lock-down for the duration.

I distinctly remember being shocked at this. Was this normal? Was it a regular occurrence in public schools?

How on Earth was any kid supposed to concentrate on their studies if drugs were either that big of a problem at the school, or else were not and the police were just so excessively vigilant?

Either way, it seemed a bit much.

Proficiency Tests

On another occasion I was at that same public high school in Hillsboro for a 10th grade proficiency test. The state of Ohio required this of homeschoolers in order for them to graduate high school.

So, there I was, a local homeschooler in Mr. Alexander's classroom, taking the test. And I was surrounded by public-school students in a public-school classroom for the first time in my life.

Prior to this, I will confess. I had for years felt insecure about being homeschooled. For some reason, I assumed my public-school peers would be smarter, more disciplined, and harder working than I was. They spent 8-hours a day in school and I never took that long. If I were getting my assignments done in 4 hours, would they be twice as smart and disciplined as I was? It sounds silly now in hindsight. But that was honestly my thought-process at the time.

In any event, this particular insecurity was annihilated the day I took my 10th grade proficiency test for the state of Ohio.

When I was finished, I double-checked my answers with the time I had left. But as I double-checked, I glanced around. Were the other kids doing likewise? No.

The students behind and beside me were all goofing off or else staring at the walls or ceiling, making little balls of paper to throw at one another, tapping and fidgeting incessantly, or trying to whisper to one another.

Why were they not more concerned with getting high marks?

When the time expired, I delivered my test to Mr. Alexander. And he told me how much he appreciated my being so "conscientious" and dutiful. He would love to have me in his tennis class if I ever attended Hillsboro High School.

Flattering as Mr. Alexander's compliments were, I realized then and there how thankful I was to not attend a public school.

The distractions were constant. Some kids paid attention; the majority seemed hell-bent not to. But it occurred to me then and there, on that day more than any other, that American public schools are not conducive environments for learning.

The 8-hours kids across the nation spend in them Monday through Friday are not spent as productively as they could be.

Hurry Up and Wait

Suppose you are a quick student at a given subject – math, for instance. You finish your work quickly and would be ready to move on. But most of the rest of the class is still working on something you wrapped up 10-minutes ago.

Now you are bored. And in your boredom, perhaps you get yourself into a little trouble. As a result of getting in trouble, you are distracted from learning the next thing you were supposed to once the rest of the class catches up.

Or maybe you do not get into trouble, but you are held back all the same from progressing until the rest of your class catches up. And the fact of you sitting there idle, tapping your fingers, and trying to sit quiet – this still serves to put your heart and mind into stagnation more than rest.

Whether or not you are getting into "trouble" is beside the point to the larger problem. This is not a natural or productive way for children to spend their time.

For another entirely realistic hypothetical on the opposite end of the spectrum, suppose you are struggling with a certain subject. For some reason, the instructions and explanations just have not made sense. You need to go over the exercises again a second and third time before you grasp the material. You look around. It looks like the rest of the class picked up what they needed to quicker than you did, and they are ready to move on.

Sorry about your luck, particularly if what you needed to learn just now was foundational to what you will be learning the rest of this year in this subject, or in the years to come.

Collectivist utilitarianism comes into play here. And the quote from Star Trek's Mr. Spock comes to mind.

"The needs of the many outweigh the needs of the few, or the one."

If only you could get the undivided attention of your teacher for a little longer. But he or she has a classroom full of other students. It would not be fair or reasonable to spend all day helping you.

Besides, you are going to get made fun of if you are either lagging behind or surging ahead of everyone. So, you had best aim for mediocrity. Settle into the middle of the pack so as not to draw unwanted attention to yourself. You just need to keep your head down and get through. Think of it like boot camp.

Education is something to endure on your way to something more important. You do not really need to fully understand the material. You just need to know enough to pass the quizzes and tests, write the essays, and complete enough projects on time to get through the class. After all, your teachers, the principle, the superintendent, the school district – everyone is depending on your standardized test scores looking competitive, at least on paper. Don't you go messing things up for everyone else. Their outstanding educator of the year award is riding on you.

Also, you would not want to disappoint your parents with bad grades. Then again, maybe you do not care about that. It depends on who your parents are and whether they think your education is terribly important, or whether they have held onto the same attitude you are forming when they too adopted it in their schooldays.

In the end, all of this is really about getting a piece of paper that says you followed all the rules and colored inside the lines like were told to.

This is about proving your capacity to follow instructions, go with the flow, and be a good little boy or girl.

With that piece of paper in hand, you can move on to making money and getting where you want to with your career and life.

Ladies and gentlemen, this is "the real world" of public education. And this is what it is all about for too many of the people calling the shots in the public schools. Subsequently, that is also what it is about for most of the students being taught in that system.

Granted, not all teachers and administrators have the mindset I just painted a picture of for you. And not all students do either.

Yet there is no denying that the ones who do have this dysfunctional mindset are able to affect a great deal of disruption in the academic pursuits of those who do not.

And if that disruption is an evil thing – which I certainly believe it is – I disagree that it is a necessary evil.

But even in the case of a classroom full of kids who earnestly want to learn the material and do well, and one teacher who genuinely wants their charges to comprehend and apply the lessons being taught, the dynamic is less than ideal.

Suppose the teacher has a class of twenty children. He cannot give individual attention to all twenty kids all the time. Some kids will pick the material up easily without much or any help. Others will struggle mightily even when given lots of attention. The majority in the middle will get the majority of lesson-planning and lesson delivery attention.

The majority of the kids will be on the mind of the good teacher who is doing his level best as he is deciding how to explain the material to everyone so that the maximum amount of good is accomplished given what he has to work with.

But pause the tape and zoom out for a moment. Therein lies the question. Do you see it?

It is there! Right there!

What has this good teacher been given to work with?

By that question, I am not talking about the children. I am asking what are the constraints and circumstances and framework he must operate within and according to? And are all of these constraints, circumstances, and frameworks fixed, immutable, and unchangeable things? Or, if they are less than ideal, or could be improved, is it possible to modify them?

The truth is simple and in the affirmative. Most of these are not fixed, immutable, and unchangeable features unless we are damned determined for them to be.

And by that, I mean to remind you of what this book is about. This is why we homeschool: to alter and adapt education to best suit the particular needs and situation of our children.

Would it not be wonderful to be able to decrease the student to teacher ratio to where more American children were able to get individual attention when they were struggling with a given subject?

Would it not be great if there were fewer unnecessary distractions and disruptions from other peoples' bad attitudes and behavior so greater attention could be paid by our children to learning the actual subjects?

The answer is yes. It would be wonderful.

It would be great. Yet it need not only be hypothetical and imaginary. It can be.

This choice really is ours.

Are we tired of drugs in schools? Have we had enough of teen pregnancy? What about peer pressure coercing our children to make other bad life choices?

We must settle for none of these things. And though there is no shortage of people campaigning to rectify these problems within the public-school system, and though that is admirable and praiseworthy, and I am not here to condemn those people, I cannot help but offer a reminder.

At the end of the day, there is a much easier way to tackle these challenges, and that is by being proactive rather than reactive.

An ounce of prevention is worth a pound of cure.

Assessing the public education system as it is, we conclude it is not a conducive environment for education. And when I say conducive, I do not mean to suggest we are dealing with an all or nothing.

Yet if by degrees some methods and modes of education are more conducive than others, and if we have established that there are more conducive educational environments – like homeschooling, for instance – by contrast, we might as well say that public education is not conducive at all in its present state.

If we can do better, we should do better. And we should not leave our children in the public schools in the vain hope that perhaps somehow, some day it will get better than it is.

If our house were on fire, we would not remain in it on the presumption – however true – that the fire will either eventually burn itself out or be put out by the fire fighters.

And this is why we homeschool.

Chapter 7

The Hand That Rocks the Cradle

"The Hand That Rocks the Cradle Is the Hand That Rules the World," a poem by William Ross Wallace, was first published in 1865 under the title "What Rules the World." Now imagine with me. What if the sentiments contained in this poem saw a revival of interest and appreciation in our day?

"Blessing on the hand of woman!
    Angels guard her strength and grace;
In the cottage, palace, hovel!
    O, no matter where the place!
Would that never storms assailed it;
    Rainbows ever gently curled;
For the hand that rocks the cradle
    Is the hand that rules the world.

Infancy's the tender fountain;

> *Power may with beauty flow,*

Mothers first to guide the streamlet,

> *From them souls unresting grow.*

Growing on for good or evil,

> *Sunshine streamed or darkness hurled;*

For the hand that rocks the cradle

> *Is the hand that rules the world.*

Women, how divine your mission

> *Here upon our natal sod;*

Keep, O keep the younger heart open

> *Always to the breath of God!*

All true trophies of the ages

> *Are from mother love impearled;*

For the hand that rocks the cradle

> *Is the hand that rules the world.*

Blessings on the hand of women!

> *Fathers, sons and daughters cry,*

And the sacred song is mingled

> *With the worship of the sky-*

Mingled where no tempest darkens,
Rainbows evermore are curled!
For the hand that rocks the cradle
Is the hand that rules the world.

What did the early feminists think of it? Surely it was still fairly well-known in their day, seeing as how the poem's refrain has been passed down to us in the present as a proverb.

Perhaps in 1865 the rumblings of discontent which eventually turned into what we now know of as feminism were already being heard from women who felt the role of mother was a waste of their time and potential.

And who knows? Perhaps that is part of why Wallace wrote the poem. I would like to imagine so, at least.

In any event, writing now in the 21st century and looking back on what feminism has wrought in American society, a tragic dismissal of the critical role of parents in general, but motherhood in particular is obvious.

Yes, we celebrate mothers and fathers. Two days are set aside for them every year. Sermons are preached in our churches. Flowers and multitools are bought and gifted to them along with cards and letters extolling the virtues of our parents – at least in some quarters.

And yet it is hard to argue, and even harder for at least me to believe, that parenthood in general or motherhood in particular are highly esteemed or honored in American society in the year 2020.

At this point, I could cite abortion statistics. We could consider again how many marriages end in divorce. You could look at how few young American men and women are getting married and having children to begin with. But all of those numbers tell us what we already know in our hearts well enough without dry data devoid of emotional weight.

As Josef Stalin is often quoted as having said:

"A single death is a tragedy; a million deaths is a statistic."

I will therefore spare you the numbers so as to not distract from the visceral reality on the personal level.

The sober truth is that many if not most Americans have increasingly seen marriage and parenthood in general, but motherhood in particular, as an impediment rather than fulfillment of their potential. Having children is seen as a nuisance and distraction from better things.

A young woman announces her plans to marry young and is immediately waylaid with calls to reconsider whether she has really had a chance to live her life yet. This carries with it the unspoken but undeniable implication that her life is over once she says, 'I do.'

Or, at a minimum, a critically important and fun part of that woman's life is over. Her fate is sealed. It is all downhill from here.

And if she starts to have children right away, and if she has more than one or two children within a few years of marriage, this point is driven home even more emphatically.

Does she not know how that happens?

She has her hands full.

That is crazy!

This was the depressing experience of my wife Lauren when we announced in the summer of 2006 our intention to marry. She was approached privately by a number of people – not just even, but especially in our little First Baptist Church in small-town Hillsboro, Ohio. She was encouraged to reconsider.

We were both in college back then. And she was asked point-blank why she should settle for me, her high school sweetheart, when she could date around? She had a nursing degree to finish. And in the meantime, there were plenty of single young men to have fun with. She should shop around. One older man even had the gall to pull her aside at her bridal shower to tell her it was not too late to change her mind!

When Lauren ignored such advice and married me anyway, and when we announced in 2007, 2008, 2009, and 2011 that we were pregnant with our first four sons, the criticisms turned to cold apathy and ostracization.

Gradually, the comments from people we knew were less and less directed at her directly and heard more second-hand. Yet even strangers we met said the same things.

> *"Don't you know how that happens?"*
> *"It looks like you have your hands full!"*
> *"Wow! That's crazy!"*

At the grocery store, the mall, Walmart, new churches we visited for the first time – any and every place, really – the response to our young and growing family was the same. Perhaps one in ten persons seemed genuinely happy for us or content to praise more than mock us.

The culmination came when our son Enoch was born in 2015. I posted a photo of our baby boy on Facebook. Someone Lauren and I had known in high school, and who my mother had taught piano lessons to commented on the photo with just two words:

"Birth Control."

We can only assume that these people were either unfamiliar with Wallace's poem or else immune to its charms.

What Happened

At this point, perhaps you are scratching your head. This is all interesting trivia, to be sure. But what do the comments we have heard about our marriage and family planning have to do with the subject of homeschooling?

The answer is that they have everything to do with one another.

Reverse engineer the problem as it now stands. Most American parents do not feel confident, competent, or especially enthusiastic about teaching their own children at home. And whether this is the cause or the effect or both, most American parents for the past century have sent their children to be educated in public schools.

We have elsewhere talked about why parents do not feel especially confident and competent. And much of this has to do with the government monopoly on education, particularly the unionized part of that monopoly. The academic elites have worked diligently to persuade parents they do not have what it takes. Leave childhood development to the professionals.

But besides this, many parents simply do not care to teach their own children at home.

Arguments about the wonders of homeschooling fall on deaf ears with such folks because they already have made up their mind about what they want in life.

You therefore cannot start the discussion off with talking them into homeschooling, therefore. You have to back up and ask the question of why they do not want to teach their children at home even if it can be demonstrated and argued that such would be far healthier and more productive for their children and their family.

Why is this?

Here now you can say that these parents disagree that homeschooling would actually be best for their children, whatever clever arguments I may find personally compelling. Perhaps many of these are single-parent families. The one parent – mother or father – has to work. They cannot afford to stay home and teach their children.

But there you have it. Can you not see?

Those prior attitudes toward marriage in the vast majority of cases determined the current single-parent home status in the majority of cases. Children were born out of wedlock. Or else the mother and father got a divorce. These two situations account for the majority of circumstances in single-parent homes in America. And now we hear that homeschooling is not a viable option.

But even if there are two parents in the home, the family has grown accustomed to both parents working. And this is another kind of problem.

We have denigrated the role of mother – as Wallace described it, "the hand that rocks the cradle."

Feminism has convinced us that the mother must emulate the father in order to earn our respect and esteem. Far from elevating the position of the woman – in the home and in society – this has served to invalidate and treat contemptuously her traditional and natural contribution to the development of children, the formation of families, the well-being of communities, and the composition of society.

It is little wonder that in a society where married mothers and fathers are scolded and ridiculed for having "too many" children, most mothers and fathers conclude they should not throw good money after bad when it comes to rearing however many children they now have – children who by God's grace somehow successfully ran the gauntlet of contraceptives, natural family planning, abortion, and vasectomies.

For the same reasons, my wife was encouraged to shop around rather than marrying me fresh out of high school. For the same reasons both of us were told we were crazy for having so many children so soon after marrying. For the same reasons, parents are discouraged from homeschooling their children. In all of the above, the claim is taken for granted by virtue of being du jour and in keeping with the Zeitgeist. Such choices detract from "reaching your full potential."

And what is meant by full potential is that young men and women should go out and get an impressive degree from a good school.

They should land a prestigious job in a respectable field. Buy and furnish a nice house. Drive a new car. Take vacations which will make for popular Instagram posts. Build up an impressive 401k.

Sweet dreams are made of these. Who am I to disagree? This is how broader society defines living the good life.

And where does marriage and having children fit into that? Where does rearing and educating the children you do have fit into that?

If we cannot find a convenient, easy, no-fuss place to squeeze those things in, then we leave them on the threshing floor to the best of our abilities until they become easy. Or else we find our opportunity to check those self-actualization boxes slipping away from us in our mid-30's to early 40's. And that is when it is considered time to "settle down."

We had our fun. Now we are tired. Our children can have whatever remains of our time, energy, and financial wherewithal – if it pleases us.

Yet what is lost in all this self-indulgent short-term thinking is what kind of real world we create for ourselves when children raised by parents who have embraced this mindset themselves grow up and have similar decisions to make.

The two children a typical American marriage produces reach adulthood and find that their parents are divorced and self-centered. They realize they were little more than an accessory or pet to the self-absorbed vision their parents had for themselves. And why get married to begin with if the odds of an unhappy divorce are so high? Why have children at all if those children are going to serve as little more than either pets or detractors from self-actualization?

But if those two children end up getting married and having children anyway, despite their own parents' poor example, they are forlorn and lost. They make it up as they go. They think they are doing well even just to get married and start a family at all in this climate. In this way, the bar is set so low that just not getting divorced and pretending at a modicum of enduring happiness will see them congratulated as a very great success.

In such an environment where family dynamics are graded on the kind of curve which presently exists, homeschooling is a big ask. It is a tall order.

But ask yourself this: if Wallace was right, who really rules the world if we are not getting married and having children, or if once we do have children we are shipping them off to someone and *something* else for rearing?

The hand that rocks the cradle is the hand that rules the world.

And this is why we homeschool.

Chapter 8

Plato, Frederick, John, And You

My maternal grandmother was Nancy Sarah Ranew. A nationally acclaimed public-school teacher in Milton, Florida for three decades, I gathered from all the stories she told me over the years that she was quite fond of teaching science, particularly biology.

Right up to when Grandma Ranew passed away in the summer of 2020, she still from time to time encountered former students at the grocery store and shopping mall. Excitedly they hugged her and said things like,

"Thank you, Mrs. Ranew, for making me do my homework. Thank you for being such a good teacher to me when I was a kid."

My Grandma Ranew often reflected fondly on her time as a teacher. She was obviously proud of her impact on the many students she taught throughout her career, and she clearly found education rewarding besides just serving as a source of income.

Despite that fact, just as often as she told me about her decades of service as a public-school teacher, my Grandma Ranew also told me how proud she was of my wife and I for homeschooling, and how proud she was of her other grandchildren – my cousins on that side of the family who were also homeschooling their children. As a seasoned and successful professional educator herself, she clearly felt that how well our children and families were doing was proof of the efficacy of home education.

What is more, Grandma Ranew told me in no uncertain terms that public education is not what it used to be. She derided Common Core and the sexual perversion and moral confusion promoted in public schools across the country.

Despite her long career in public education, Grandma Ranew was so glad we were not sending her great-grandchildren into that environment. She celebrated that we were protecting our children from the many dangerous influences which have become intimately associated with a system she once worked so hard within.

Perhaps you do not descend from educators like I do. However, if you are an American, your grandparents and parents probably also attended public schools like my parents and grandparents did. And by the numbers, chances are high that you and most of the people you know followed also in the footsteps of your parents and grandparents in sending their children after them to be educated in the same way they themselves were educated.

By the numbers, your children probably either currently attend public schools or else are expected to when they are old enough. So many Americans have attended public schools for so many generations that public education seems now for many a tradition as American as apple pie and baseball.

But how much do you really know about the history of the institution?

Would it surprise you to learn that public schools being used as a means of social engineering – for implanting dedication to certain political values and assumptions – is not at all either a recent development or an accidental one?

No, the social engineering scheme in public education did not start under President Barack Obama's administration, nor even in just the last century for that matter. American public schools being used as a tool of controlling and manipulating the masses ultimately traces its intellectual roots back to Greece in the fourth century B.C.

American Exceptionalism Embraces the Prussian Model

In 1918, Richard Thomas Alexander – professor of elementary education at George Peabody College for Teachers, and an early proponent of John Dewey's progressive education movement in the U.S. – made an important study of the Prussian educational system and expressed some unsettling summary remarks on the nature of that system:

"The Prussian citizen cannot be free to do and act for himself; that the Prussian is to a large measure enslaved through the medium of his school; that his learning instead of making him his own master forges the chain by which he is held in servitude; that the whole scheme of the Prussian elementary school education is shaped with the express purpose of making ninety-nine out of every one hundred citizens subservient . . . The elementary schools of Prussia have been fashioned so as to make spiritual and intellectual slaves of the lower classes."

– The Prussian Elementary Schools by Richard Thomas Alexander, PhD

Now one might expect from reading such a summary that even just the idea of this Prussian system of schooling would be intolerable and anathema to the American people, who value and cherish liberty, freedom, and independence above all other virtues.

We are, after all, "the land of the free and the home of the brave." Surely we Americans could never be made to embrace a system designed to make slaves out of *"ninety-nine of every one hundred"* of us.

Yet for some reason and purpose, the founding fathers of our present-day American public education system chose to emulate rather than avoid the Prussian model as they assembled America's version of it, all the while admitting things like:

"Numerous tracts were issued from the English press . . . strongly denouncing the whole plan of education in Prussia, as being not only designed to produce, but as actually producing, a spirit of blind acquiescence to arbitrary power, in things spiritual as well as temporal – as being in fine, a system of education adapted to enslave, and not to enfranchise, the human mind."

– Horace Mann, as quoted in Cubberley, 1920

As Yehudi Meshchaninov at the New American Academy summarizes in his 2012 paper, *The Prussian-Industrial History of Public Schooling*, America chose to make its own army of educational bureaucrats in imitation of the Prussian model.

"Educrats" were to be a new kind of teacher serving as cogs in an intensely hierarchical and centralized machine fueled by fear and isolation.

Personal initiative and independent decision-making were dismissed in favor of teaching obedience and unquestioning submission to authority.

Subjects were to be taught without context or concern for the genuine comprehension by students of their interconnected implications.

This, not accidentally, was from the programme's inception designed to stunt intellectual growth and rigor for the vast majority of students expected to live out their days serving the greater good as menial labor in our factories or soldiers in our armies.

Emphasis in this educational system was to be placed on useful conformity and submission over genuine or meaningful learning in anything approaching the classical sense.

Students were to obey their teachers. Teachers in turn would obey their principals. And principals would obey their superintendents, et cetera, on up the chain all the way to the top.

Frederick the Great's Obedience Factory

To get a clearer picture of what the Prussian educational system America adopted was really like, consider the professed philosophy of Prussia's monarch, Frederick the Great.

It was Frederick the Great and his father, Frederick William I, who were responsible for devising and instituting this system in Prussia. And a glimpse of their mindset reinforces rather than undermines the view of that system as being one designed for control and manipulation of the masses rather than legitimate education.

Reigning from 1740 to 1786, some of Frederick the Great's most famous gems include:

"An educated people can be easily governed."

"If my soldiers were to begin to think, not one would remain in the ranks."

"It seems to me that man is made to act rather than to know: the principles of things escape our most persevering researches."

"Religion is the idol of the mob; it adores everything it does not understand."

Notice a common theme?

Unquestioning obedience to command, unfettered and unrestrained by the limitations which comprehension, agreement, or religious conviction might present – these were the primary values of Frederick the Great where education and government were concerned.

To put it another way, education in Prussia was a means to an end for Frederick William II and his father. The governed masses – especially the soldiers – were needed as pawns in larger and more complex governmental plans and purposes.

The public schools of Prussia were therefore designed with a kind of rigid industrialized utility to serve as the psychological and spiritual factories for mass-producing hearts and minds ready to obey.

In short, the Prussian public education system consolidated imperial power and produced good soldiers who obeyed orders to kill or be killed rather than questioning either the morality or wisdom of their commanders' decisions or retreating from what they had deemed was an unjust cause for shedding blood – either their own or someone else's.

"Focusing on following directions, basic skills, and conformity, he sought to indoctrinate the nation from an early age. Isolating students in rows and teachers in individual classrooms fashioned a strict hierarchy— intentionally fostering fear and loneliness."

– The Prussian-Industrial Model

Back in the 18th century, Frederick the Great's Prussia gives us an example of a European monarch embracing a thoroughly Platonic ideal of government as educator with the utmost commitment and conviction.

But the intellectual seeds which sprouted in Frederick the Great's Prussia, and which were thereafter transplanted to America by John Dewey and others, were originally sown in ancient Greece.

Plato's Utopian Vision for Public Education

In the works of Plato – *Laws* and *Republic* – the Greek philosopher presented an ideal form of government in which children are taken from their parents in their formative years and instructed in how to think rationally about the world as it is, apart from superstitions and fables about heroes and gods which were to Plato likened to the distorted shadows of things on a cave wall rather than the real things themselves seen directly in open daylight.

According to Plato, the government rather than parents should be seen as possessing the primary authority over and responsibility for children, and should cultivate in the children of their society:

> *"...A keen desire to become a perfect citizen who knows how to rule and be ruled."*
> **– Plato's Laws, bk. 1, 643**

As Plato's theory went, such a society in which his ideas were embraced and implemented would enjoy more harmony and social cohesion when the feelings of love, devotion, and trust children traditionally reserved for their parents were instead transferred to the civil government and broader society.

> *"In the Republic Plato abolishes the family for the guardians, to avoid nepotism and amassing of private wealth (Republic, bk. 5, 464). Wives and children are to be held in common by all, and no parent is to know his own child nor any child his parents–" provided it can be done" (Republic, bk. 5, 457). In the Laws Plato allows family raising for all citizens, with restrictions on child rearing and inheritance (Laws, bk. 5, sec.729)." (FAQ.org)*

According to Plato, once everyone was on the same page and knew how to think rationally, society would enjoy the inevitable blessings of good decision-making, cooperation, and prosperity.

Indeed, we know these ideas were not merely theoretical. The Utopian vision Plato outlined was the very same scheme rulers such as Frederick the Great attempted to realize throughout history, even up to and including our day.

But the problems with educating children and engineering society in this manner should be obvious.

A nation of slaves subjected to bait-and-switch tactics where they and their children are promised a quality education, then given drills on how to obey their government as its unquestioning slaves – this could reasonably be expected to leave such peoples vulnerable to the amoral whims and cruelty of strongmen, dictators, and tyrants.

Again, this is not mere theory or hypothetical imagining. It has been argued with merit that these vulnerabilities inherent to the Prussian model of public education were why Germany fell prey to Adolf Hitler and the Nazis in the early 20th century.

The deleterious effects of the Prussian educational system on the ability of the German people to question authority or for individual citizens to possess and follow their own internal moral compass were still being felt 200 years after Frederick the Great and his father first hoisted that method of social engineering and population control on the masses they governed.

Even a cursory examination of what the Nazis did with Germany's public schools once they came to power proves that Hitler apprehended the principle that he who controls and shapes the children of a society will effectively dictate that society's future.

As an aside, it is worth noting that some Germans recognized this hazard.

Famed pastor, theologian, and martyr Dietrich Bonhoeffer hailed from a family in which public education was seen as morally and spiritually dangerous.

For this reason, Dietrich's earliest education was homeschooling, and it is not hard to see how home education predicated on a healthy distrust of blind, absolute obedience to the authority of the German state in all things equipped Dietrich to strongly oppose the Nazis in adulthood.

Though defiance of the Nazis ultimately cost Bonhoeffer his life, he is widely regarded as a hero of those dark days in Germany – and rightly so.

Chapter 9

But God Entrusted Children to Fathers and Mothers

I find deeply disturbing the thought of my children being manipulated into unquestioning loyalty, obedience, and subservience to the State, and you should too. Regardless what machinations Plato or Frederick the Great or John Dewey or any of their modern-day contemporaries have worked tirelessly to theorize and implement for the supposedly "greater good" of society as a whole, I read in God's Word that I as a father and my wife as a mother are the ones who are called to:

"Train up a child in the way he should go; even when he is old he will not depart from it."
– Proverbs 22:6

Subsequently, all parents – but Christian parents especially – have a responsibility to ask a critically important question here. Does the American public education system train up our children in the way they should go?

And can or should we in good conscience make ourselves content depending on an endless number of educrats, politicians, and special interest groups, relying on that invisible conglomeration to decide in our place for so much of our sons' and daughters' childhoods what the way they should go will be?

I for one cannot in good conscience send my children off to be raised by a system which not only does not fear the Lord and is not only disinclined to my children being trained up in the fear and admonition of the Lord, but which is even increasingly hostile to those aims.

The good news is that I do not have to place my blind trust in the educrats of the American public education system. God gave my children to me to be their father, not so I could hand them off to the State.

And this is why we homeschool.

As it is written,

"Children obey your parents in the Lord, for this is right. "Honor your father and mother" (this is the first commandment with a promise), "that it may go well with you and that you may live long in the land." Fathers, do not provoke your children to anger, but bring them up in the discipline and instruction of the Lord."
– Ephesians 6:1-4

Notice what this passage does not say. It does not say "children obey the government," or "honor the State." Nor does it say "Governments... bring your children up in the discipline and instruction of obeying you unquestioningly."

The simple fact is that God did not bless my wife and I with children just so we could serve as middlemen passing them off to a State which all too often sees the expansion of its own power and control over the daily affairs of its citizens as not a means to an end, but as a legitimate end unto itself.

My parents trained and educated my brother and I at home. Lauren and I can train and educate our children at home.

And again, this is why we homeschool.

Homeschool Your Children

Everyone I meet who has any involvement in or dependence upon American public schools seems to believe their local school is the exception to the rule. Whatever the condition of every other school in the country, or of the overarching public education system, their local school is somehow free of all that.

This does not really surprise me. It does stand to reason.

If parents did not believe their local branch of the public education system was tolerable, how on Earth could they entrust their children to it?

Now listen. If you are an American man or woman who attended public schools and whose children are also, and if you have not closed this book by now, offended by my challenging assertions and questions, please hear me when I say that my intention is not to malign your sincere love for your children.

I know you love your children and I trust that you want what is best for them. You send your children off to public schools because you genuinely believe that is what is in their best interest, all things considered.

It is true that my conscience does not permit me to support the public schools or send my children into them. I see the larger public education system as corrupt and godless. How then could I in good conscience send my children to be educated by it?

Yet my good conscience also does not permit me to go farther than I ought in suggesting you are an evil scoundrel if you still strive to make that corrupt, imperfect system work for the good of your children while honoring God and following Jesus in it.

We are called to be in the world but not of it, you may rightly point out.

I blink in writing this and imagine you may be a hardworking Christian teacher in a school you believe is still exceptional, which still holds to much of the traditional goodness your grandparents recounted to you fondly about their schooldays. This I beg of you: please do not take offense as though I am dismissing all your hard work with this candid summary of the system in which you work.

I blink again and imagine another scenario. Perhaps you are not a teacher. Perhaps you are a Christian parent sending your children to a small local school in your hometown.

Everyone knows everyone and the school has served as a hub for the community for untold generations. You know all your child's teachers and classmates. In fact, you went to school with or are related to everyone who runs the school now.

If such is the case, please do not be baffled or hurt by my suggestion that your local school is nevertheless a part of something larger which is not so wholesome as you doubtless want to believe.

As I told you in the previous chapter, my grandmother was a public-school teacher for decades. She told me American public schools are much worse now than they were back when she was teaching.

And listen, you parents and teachers who take offense at what I am saying: My grandmother was one of you long before either you or I were born. She said the system is not what it used to be and that she was glad her grandchildren were homeschooling her great-grandchildren rather than sending them into that mess.

So, if you do not believe me, believe her. But if you will not believe her, who will you believe?

The answer is that you will believe no one about these things, no matter their credibility or the strength of their arguments, if you insist on imitating the three wise monkeys – Mizaru, Kikazaru, and Iwasaru – who see no evil, hear no evil, and speak no evil.

Who's Driving Now?

Ah, but wait. You have another objection. If you were paying attention to the brief history I just laid out, you are confused now.

Did I not just trace the roots of the American public education system all the way back through Prussia and Frederick the Great to Greece and Plato?

Did I not just claim through this brief history lesson that the American public education system as a whole has been fundamentally misguided since it was first put in place?

Yes, I did. I did indeed say that. I still am saying that.

The truth is that well before my grandmother started teaching, the present system was designed and implemented to churn out children of whom the vast majority would someday work as obedient, acquiescent laborers in factories and soldiers in armies – slaves either way to a centralized government and all its notions of "the greater good."

But if all of that is true, then why would I or my grandmother claim the system is more of a problem now than it was when my grandmother was teaching?

To answer that question, I would say that the journey of a thousand miles begins with a single step. And the fact that we are now more clearly arriving at an unpleasant destination should inspire us to look back and recognize that we have been traveling in this direction for some time to get where we are.

I would also ask you to consider who in recent years has been allowed to sit in the driver's seat of this vehicle that was intended from its inception to take everyone in it to this same place.

Who is our Frederick the Great atop this intensely hierarchical social engineering machine?

Who is our Plato, and what is his philosophy for the American people?

And if this American public education system is just one great, big, industrialized monstrosity, who is telling the cogs which direction they must rotate and how fast? And who is telling them all how they must behave now?

What is the larger agenda?

Perhaps you take comfort in being a Christian teacher yourself or knowing that your child's teachers are Christians. But look at this honestly and without the veneer of wishful thinking.

The amount of resistance a local Christian teacher can put up against orders coming down from higher up in the chain of command is really rather small. And at a certain point, we know from experience that those local Christian teachers who disobey and make a fuss are soon enough removed from their post and replaced with more obedient substitutes.

Consequently, many Christian teachers make note of the line they cannot cross and give it as wide a berth as job security requires, thereby mitigating and dampening their effectiveness even as they strive to maximize the same by remaining in their current position.

The unvarnished truth is that our present-day American public education system was patterned after the Prussian example – both on purpose and for a purpose. It was designed and deployed to drill unquestioning obedience and subservience to the government into children from a young age. This necessitated an utter disregard, and even contempt for the genuine education, intellectual growth, or ability to take personal initiative and make decisions independently. Such things serving as counterproductive to the desired ends of the powers that be, these personal qualities had to be systematically stamped out of children's hearts and minds before they could embrace an adequately subservient attitude and mindset.

And such was never going to be true only with the students obeying the teachers. No, it was always going to include the teachers obeying their principals. It was always going to require the principals obeying their superintendents, et cetera on up the chain of command – both as a way of maintaining discipline and uniformity, but also as a way of modeling the desired sort of submission to hierarchy for the children and parents watching.

Not accidentally but by design, this American public education system holds in contempt the individual conscience, personal judgment, and character of your local schoolteacher when such lead to questioning or disobeying orders that are handed down from on high. In this way, hands are tied. And the conclusions are all foregone and predestined.

We can do this the easy way, or we can do this the hard way.

And this, dear reader, is why we homeschool.

And this is why I would encourage you to do so also.

Opt Out

Regardless what weird, perverted, godless, anti-Christian place the school bus driver wants to take American public schools to, we can opt out.

We can choose instead to drive ourselves and our children to somewhere better and brighter. And so we should.

My children and I need not go along for the ride and suffer fools and folly gladly.

Nor either do you and your children need to.

That is part of the beauty of homeschooling, and I believe that embracing this principle must necessarily follow when we understand God's original intention for the family.

In recent years, the mostly secular American public has grappled with what marriage and family truly mean, as well as what the purpose of the family is.

If you are like me, you have been disheartened to find society "evolving" through media and public education campaigns designed to encourage children and adults alike to either experiment sexually on their own, or else affirm others as they do so.

But remember what God's Word says about the purpose of marriage and the family.

> *"Did he not make them one, with a portion of the Spirit in their union? And what was the one God seeking? Godly offspring. So guard yourselves in your spirit and let none of you be faithless to the wife of your youth."*
> *– Malachi 2:15*

My wife and I drive the school bus in our home and family. We take the responsibility for training and educating our children and nurturing them along the way as they learn to read, write, do their arithmetic, understand science and history and any number of other things that interest and benefit them.

We get to cultivate their God-given intellects and personalities even as we train them up in the way they should go – not as godless and unquestioning slaves to any number of hair-brained agendas of yesterday, today, or tomorrow. No, the way they should go requires that they be young men and women who are bold and courageous and who embrace wisdom and goodness.

"Now therefore fear Yahweh and serve him in sincerity and in faithfulness. Put away the gods that your fathers served beyond the River and in Egypt and serve Yahweh. And if it is evil in your eyes to serve Yahweh, choose this day whom you will serve, whether the gods your fathers served in the region beyond the River, or the gods of the Amorites in whose land you dwell. But as for me and my house, we will serve Yahweh."

– Joshua 24:14-15

I hope you have made and embraced this commitment also. Yet if you have, it is possible you still believe American public schools are a viable option for training your children. If so, it is not proper for me to lambast or accuse you of false motives, or of miscarrying your responsibilities.

Yet I would encourage you, and in the strongest possible terms, insofar as wisdom and knowledge and my own conscience compel me.

See this system for what it is and make your decisions accordingly, for the sake of your children and your family, and for the sake of your posterity for generations to come.

Please know that I love and care for you with sincere brotherly affection, and that I will pray earnestly for you and your children whether you homeschool or not. Whatever your lot in life, keep in mind the words of Proverbs 4:23.

"Watch over your heart with all diligence, For from it flow the springs of life."

Those words apply not only to us as individuals watching over our own hearts, but also to all who look after children. We must watch over their hearts, knowing that from them flow the springs of life.

And this is why we homeschool.

Section III

Homeschooling

Chapter 10

Overcoming Insecurity

Many parents are convinced they could never teach their own children at home. Very few of them are correct in that persuasion. The vast majority can homeschool their children if they choose to.

But it would be no service at all to those parents to leave off there and say no more about it. And I for one am not content merely contradicting deep and pervasive insecurities.

So, let us press on past obvious admissions of the reality that many, perhaps even most parents in this country harbor deep and pervasive insecurities about training their children.

Why are these parents insecure? That is the question we ought to be asking. Moreover, are the reasons for these insecurities well-founded, or are they superfluous and unnecessary?

If we can identify the source of these insecurities, then comes another task.

We have some weighing and measuring to do. Either there is more reason for confidence than is recognized, or else there are ways of overcoming insecurity and building confidence.

The goal of an insecure person should be to overcome their insecurity where it is without merit. For all the preoccupation with personal safety in 21st century America, the lack of attention paid to internal security being based on more than mantras and medication astounds me. This is a byproduct of our often materialistic, naturalistic, and secular perspective on life.

But let us not dive into trite diatribes against consumerism here. That is not the root; it is only a branch.

And let us not rail against free market capitalism run amok. Such crusades are badly misguided, and they misapprehend the foundation of our cultural folly and decay.

The seeds of our present distress were planted centuries ago when enlightened men endeavored to set side religious dogma and doctrine in the interest of ending sectarian strife between Roman Catholics and the various tribes of Protestants in Europe.

Bloody and destructive wars of religion, wasteful and taxing power plays, and unending and contentious arguments over what measure of authority in Christian life stemmed from the Scriptures, from the Church, or from an individual conscience – all of these wearied a great many intelligent and learned men who at the end of the striving yearned more than anything for a modicum of peace.

Some, though by no means all of these men, chose unwisely to renounce Christianity. Pursuing science, art, and philosophy rationally would allow Europe and the United States of America to make great strides in discovering ever-more clever and ingenious ways of organizing and expanding knowledge and cooperation.

Yet one of the unintended but entirely foreseeable consequences of this was that subsequent generations progressively – or regressively if you will – lost their religion. Western civilization perfected the art of putting metaphysical and spiritual convictions on the backburner to such an extent that many forgot how to integrate their belief in God into everyday decision-making.

What we short-handedly refer to as consumerism and materialism was birthed out of this forgetfulness.

Where our ancestors debated in their homes, churches, and town halls whether certain courses of action were righteous, not just practical, successive generations gave way increasingly to considering only the physical expedience of the various options available.

No more fundamental and foundational example of this can be found than in how we now came to organize and plan our families.

Family Meeting

Close your eyes and picture a young man and his wife sitting at their dining room table, discussing whether the bride should get a job.

By averages, the American family has two young children. The man works full-time and makes just barely enough to pay for necessities.

And not much is left over after that. Perhaps someday they will be able to afford a nicer car, a bigger home, a boat, and annual vacations to exciting foreign places. But they cannot do those things now, and that bothers them.

And so it goes that to close the gap between them and their material ambitions, the man and his wife are considering sending the wife into the workforce and finding someone to watch their two young children during the day while both parents work.

The woman tells her husband she wants to stay home with their children, at least until they are old enough to go to school. But the husband is adamant. Living so close to the limits of their budget causes him stress. He is preoccupied and discontented by all the things his friends and co-workers enjoy – whether or not some of them are married with children as he is, or in the same stage in their career as he is.

The man reminds his wife of all the things they could afford to buy and do if she were working as well. And she should imagine with him how much better off their children would be with nicer clothes, a bigger home and yard, and a nicer car.

She is unconvinced and cannot shake her misgivings about who would watch their children during the day. And how much would that cost – not just to cover daycare fees, but also in valuable time for bonding with her young children still in their formative years?

What Is Missed

What has been missing so often in discussions like this had all over America for decades is a consideration of the responsibility fathers and mothers have to "train up a child in the way he should go."

What has been so often absent in these deliberations has been a consideration of the emotional, intellectual, and spiritual foundation being laid in childhood.

Meanwhile, what has been so often present in abundance has been a kind of handwringing over whether parents have what it takes to properly care for their children.

Do fish in water realize they are wet? So also, we have too often failed to recognize how much value we assign to physical goods where the well-being of our families is concerned more broadly.

This is not to say that physical goods are of no consequence. As a husband and father myself, I am keenly aware of the importance and cost of food, clothing, shelter, and transportation for my wife and children and myself.

And it does not suffice to check those boxes with just any representative sample. Not all food, clothing, shelter, and transportation is created equal. We have to factor both quantity and quality into our equation. And as we increase either quantity or quality, and certainly when we combine the two, we quickly see rising costs which must be offset by an increased capacity to pay those costs.

Yet this is also true with regards to other dimensions of well-being. We are not just stomachs, so we cannot only consider food. We are not just bodies which need to be clothed, housed, and transported.

Our hearts and minds and souls must be considered as well, and not all the things which we might provide for to sustain and nourish them are equal either.

Yet it is just this sort of holistic thinking and discussion which is woefully missing so much of the time at American dinner tables because of how numb and apathetic we have become to the moral and spiritual aspects of our beings.

What is more, the same mechanic which influences us to neglect such a holistic approach to our family dynamics also causes us to feel insecure when we depart from the cultural norm in society around us and factor into our decision-making more than just the material cost-benefit analysis, particularly where stay-at-home mothering and homeschooling are concerned.

Be Conspicuous

You feel the eyes. Your face burns red with blushing.

Your extended family and friends and co-workers balk when you tell them your wife will stay home with the kids and homeschool them.

Check your neck for whether a second head has grown there based on the way they are looking at you.

They clearly do not understand your reasons. And from what you know of how they have oriented their homes and families their disagreement is tacit and entirely predictable.

The anxiety you feel about your newfound conspicuousness has a practical and physical dimension as well. What if they are offended by you making a different choice than they have? What if they start picking on your performance at work? Perhaps you do not get invited to parties and dinners like you once did. Maybe that puts a ceiling on how far your career can advance.

Once again, though, is the insecurity we feel about doing what we believe is the right thing based on a holistic approach to well-being?

You want your finances to be healthy. That is well. You want your social life to be healthy. That is good. But can either of those dimensions of your existence be healthy if the attitudes of your heart do not keep the opinions others have about you and your family in perspective?

Consider Proverbs 29:25.

"The fear of man lays a snare,
but whoever trusts in Yahweh is safe."

In other words, the first step overcoming insecurity with regards to homeschooling your child is asking how much of your insecurity stems from fear of other people disapproving. And how much of your insecurity bears any relation to trusting in God?

If in the course of honest introspection you find that your desire to buy nicer food, clothing, shelter, and transportation is based on fear that others will look down on you if you do not, do you find also that you are trusting God with these things?

And if you find that your insecurity about homeschooling your child stems from material concerns – including but not limited to how such will negatively impact your social life – where does trusting God enter into the equation?

Setting these concerns aside for a moment, what legacy are you leaving your children, and what sort of example are you setting for them if you make decisions on how to organize your home and raise your children based off dollars and cents and anxiety over what other people may think of you?

Alternatively, if you picture your child someday being your age, and sitting at their dining room table with their spouse to make a decision concerning the welfare of their home and family, what is the best you can hope for them in that moment?

When I answer this question, the best I can hope for my children is that they overcome rather than bowing to these kinds of insecurity. Moreover, I hope they do so by trusting in the Lord rather than fearing what others might think of them. That is to say, my children will have a much better legacy and example to follow in my wife and I if we choose to overcome insecurity and purely materialistic considerations for the sake of honoring God and being holistic in the way we orient our lives.

And this is why we homeschool.

Chapter 11

Homeschooling is not a one-size-fits-all option for educating your child. And that is why you should homeschool your child.

I have often heard non-homeschooling parents say that homeschooling is not for everyone. What they mean by this is that their child is different than my children. Therefore, homeschooling would not be a good fit the way that it is for my children.

Their son or daughter needs certain things in order to be happy, healthy, and well-adjusted. Socialization and sports are the two most common examples.

Public-schooling parents do not suppose these and other things their child needs can be had in the proper way or the correct amount when homeschooling. Public schooling, meanwhile, is where it is at. These things are fuller, truer, and more plentiful there. Thus, naturally, the decision to send little Johnny and Suzie to public school rather than homeschooling them.

I have often heard homeschooling parents as well saying the same thing. Homeschooling is not for everyone. This they do probably because they believe it. Having heard the saying often enough from public schooling parents, the homeschooling parents repeat what they have heard from the public schooling parents, and do not give overmuch critical thought to whether the saying is true.

But there is a deeper reason these homeschooling moms and dads say it, whether or not they themselves really believe it. To concede that homeschooling is not for everyone is an effective way of making the parents who send their children to public schools feel less threatened, offended, and standoffish.

The saying is a kind of defense mechanism if you will.

As an aside, I will let you in on a little secret. We homeschooling parents want to be your friends even if you send your children to public school. It pains us when you are angry with us because you think we look down on you for educating your children in a way we disagree with.

Anger and offense are typically not compatible with strong, lasting friendship. So, we try to head those off at the pass when we can. This is often the way and means by which we try to do that, by readily conceding that homeschooling is not for everyone.

But there is another way to look at this statement, and that is the way I look at it. So, hear me out.

One Size Fits All

First off, I agree that homeschooling is not a one-size-fits-all option for teaching children.

However, what I mean by this is something a bit different from what other people mean. What I mean is that when you homeschool your child, you as the parent get to take into consideration all the particulars of what your child needs.

You know your child struggles with certain subjects and is passionate about others.

You know whether your child is a loner or a social butterfly who never tires of being around and talking with other people.

Perhaps your child is a straight arrow, never misbehaving in any discernable way. Or maybe they are a troublemaker, always up to mischief and misadventures. Either way, you know them.

Maybe your child loves sports, and lives to play them with their friends, especially for an audience.

Or maybe your child loves music and cannot imagine life without the band, orchestra, or choir they make music with.

Now consider all of this and more in light of the fact that homeschooling is what we make it.

When you homeschool, you give your child the strategic individual attention needed to help them overcome their areas of difficulty.

But there is more. Look on the bright side.

What does your child need in order to thrive where their natural interests lie?

Your child positively adoring some subjects and pursuits means you can help them dive deeper into those than they would have the opportunity to in a conventional public education.

Educating them at home, you as the parent pick and choose supplemental resources which help your son or daughter go farther and faster. This makes the most of their innate interests.

That old saying "strike while the iron is hot" applies here. But you also know not just when the iron is hot. You know where it is hot.

If your child is a loner in the public schools, is that because they are not learning socialization so much as anti-social tendencies from other kids? Do they get picked on or excluded in a mean-spirited way?

If so, homeschooling might just be the ticket to deliver them from these unnecessary and corrosive woes.

If your child is being picked on in the public schools, your child would welcome liberation from the unhealthy relationships they feel trapped by right now.

Perhaps that liberation would help them to learn not to hate associating with people whom they have come to associate with bullying and mistreatment.

Is your child a straight arrow and you worry they will become a goody-two-shoes? Homeschool them and work on the cultivation of genuine virtue for more than just the sake of appearances.

If they are mischievous and a troublemaker, homeschool them and observe more closely their tendency to get into trouble. Perhaps they are dying of boredom on the inside. This is their cry for help.

Homeschooling gives you more hours in a day with which to consistently redirect your child into considerate and responsible activities that more fully engage their creative and imaginative faculties.

But what about sports and music? You worry your child will not learn how to play well with others if they are stuck with you all day.

Again, homeschooling is what we make it.

If you want your child to play sports, that is not at all impossible. On the contrary, more efficient ways of completing the academic part of their education leave more time in the day free for exercise and practice.

In the places I have lived, there have always been leagues which are open to homeschooled children if you look for them. Or, if they do not yet exist, why not band together with other homeschooling parents and create those leagues?

This applies also to music. The homeschooling groups I was a part of growing up in the 90's and early 2000's had choirs and bands.

And as with sports, more time-effective completion of academic pursuits leaves more time in the day freed up to learn and practice instruments and music theory.

But why stop there? If your child loves music, encourage them to write and compose music, or to record and mix it on their computer.

Where There Is A Will

Freedom can be scary, but it is also essential. Creativity and problem-solving cannot exist without freedom. Yes, liberty can be overwhelming in combination with uncharted territory and a multitude of options. But it can also be exciting if we choose to see it that way. And we should so choose.

One of the major reasons my wife Lauren and I homeschool our children is because of the freedom it affords our family to do, be, and become who and what we believe God created us for.

There are challenges with homeschooling, to be sure. Just so, there are challenges to raising children in general, no matter how we choose to have ours educated.

But imagine the possibilities of venturing forth with a commitment to freedom, creativity, and problem-solving. Feel those goosebumps up your arms and back at the thought that your child could do more than mundanely checking standardized boxes based on an artificially one-size-fits-all approach to education.

In the public schools, children's hearts and minds are too often regarded as a kind of uniform raw material destined for mass-produced output. But our children are – each and every one of them – one-of-a-kind and uniquely suited individuals. And the way we educate them should reflect that. Moreover, the way we educate our children can reflect that.

Born for Such A Time as This

Personally, I can think of few things as impactful on encouraging my children to pursue their calling in life than choosing as their father an educational option which recognizes that they have a special part to play in human history.

Esther's uncle Mordecai tells her in the Old Testament book we know by her name, "You were born for such a time as this." And that is a positively beautiful sentiment. What is more, though, that positively beautiful statement is something we should embrace in the way we bring up our children. It is something we should tell our children every night as we put them to bed, just like we tell them "Sweet dreams."

And we should remind ourselves of this about our children even more often as we parent and instruct them.

The family your child was born into, including you being their parents, in the time and place they were born, with the particular combination of traits they were born with – all of these and other factors are a unique recipe which you as your child's parent are also uniquely positioned to apprehend and appreciate. So, meditate on that fact. And factor it into your decision of how to educate and prepare your sons and daughters for adulting someday.

Every child is different.

Yes, yes. Certain traits are common enough, while others are rarer but not wholly unique in and of themselves. The point is not to consider your child only in terms of their individual traits – whether strengths or weaknesses, whether rare or common. The whole is more than the sum of its parts, and this is especially true when it comes to people.

As fathers and mothers, we do well to consider not just the specific pursuits and subjects our children like and dislike, or what they are good or bad at. But how do those combinations of likes and dislikes, activities, and topics they are inclined or disinclined toward exploring and developing come together in combination to uniquely suit your son or daughter for playing some indispensable part?

As Shakespeare's Jacques puts it in As You Like It,

"All the world's a stage, and all the men and women merely players."

This conviction we want our children to carry with them through adulthood – that they were born for a purpose, and are here by God's provision and design, and according to his plans and purposes – this is what we work daily to instill in our children in the way we talk to and about them. It colors the sort of books, music, movies, and games we place in and take out of their path. And it focuses and directs the way we encourage and require them to relate to one another.

All of this is part and parcel to education, yes. But it is also possible for other philosophies of education to exist, and even to be predominate and popular, without any attention paid to this foundation.

No small part of the beauty and freedom of homeschooling is that this sentiment I am describing not only can be a part of the way we educate our children. By choosing to homeschool our children, we also are free to choose to make this sentiment central to the way our children are educated.

In other words, we should not merely make mention of this and leave it at that, like the Hallmark card you got from your aunt on your birthday. You smiled at it, thanked her, and then immediately set it aside as little more than a pleasant thought.

Yes, yes. Our children were born for a purpose and are here for a reason. But it is possible to make only a passing mention of that fact before promptly forgetting about it. We can, if we do not take care, carry on as though this is not a relevant fact.

However, by homeschooling we can also embrace this idea as crucial, critical, and central. We are free to weave it into all our instruction. We are free to dye the fabric of our family tapestry with this vibrant color.

When we make use of the freedom inherent to home education – acting accordingly, diligently, and consistently to remind ourselves and our children of this necessity – we find ourselves much more purposeful in the way we educate our children.

We talked earlier the responsibility of parents to train up their children in the way they should go so that when they are older they will not depart from it. But a major part of the way our children should go when they are older is acting on purpose, speaking on purpose, and relating to the people, places, and things around them on purpose. Before our children can do all of that, they must first start with the conviction that they themselves are here for a purpose. And we as parents can do a great deal of help or hindrance to our children believing this big idea about themselves by first believing or disbelieving it ourselves. Therefore, we should believe it. And we should plan their education accordingly.

And this is why we homeschool.

Chapter 12

When Lauren and I tell people that we homeschool, we often hear other mothers and fathers say they do not think they could homeschool because it would drive them crazy to have their children home with all day.

May I respectfully submit that if you are one of those people – afraid your children would drive you insane if they were home all day – that may actually be all the more evidence you should homeschool?

Let us be honest. At the first, you are admitting that your children are not so well-behaved as you wish they were. They do not have the manners they ought to. More to the point, they do not obey you as their father and mother as well as children should obey their parents in a perfect world.

Perhaps also, your children are undisciplined. They do not readily apply themselves to their studies. They are easily distracted. They sneak away from their homework assignments every chance they get, and do not readily follow-through when given chores and other tasks to complete.

If such is true of your children, join the club. Welcome to parenthood.

Such has been, sometimes still is, and presumably always will be to some extent true of all my children as well. So, I can relate to your frustration.

But that is not where we as parents can afford to camp out. We cannot settle for this. We cannot passively accept when our children require instruction in manners, discipline, and obedient hearts, throwing our hands up in helplessness as though there is nothing for it.

No child is born with these things innately formed already, at least not in my experience and observation. But then that is what God made parents for.

To say we do not want to homeschool our children because they lack manners, discipline, and obedience is like saying we do not want to homeschool our children because they do not yet know how to read, write, and do their math.

These are all things our children have to be taught. And if our children do not learn these things from us, who will they learn them from?

The misapprehension seems to be that parents who homeschool their children somehow got a different batch of children to start with.

Our children were born with supernatural, superhuman gifting in these areas. Most parents' children lack these things, and you either have them or you do not.

But that is just silly. And when we say such silly things out loud rather than secretly assuming them, we have to recognize just how unreasonable they really are.

Silly or no, let us ask the question out loud and consider what our honest answer really is to the question. If our children so far have not learned good manners and obedience to legitimate authority – especially parental authority – from us, who have we been expecting them to learn these things from?

The short answer to this question in all too many cases is that parents unconsciously expect their children to learn manners, discipline, and obedience to parental authority from the same place they learn reading, writing, and arithmetic.

And for many parents who send their children to the public schools, the expectation is that their children will learn all of the above in the public schools they attend.

But let us perform a quick test for whether this is actually where children learn manners, discipline, and obedience.

Consider how many children actually do learn these things in that place. And left to their own devices, how polite are public school children whose parents do not teach them etiquette at home? And by contrast, how polite is the typical homeschooled child?

Now depart the realm of the hypothetical and theoretical. Return again to the garden of the real. We all know the answer to this.

The proof of the pudding is in the tasting. And the proof of where children learn good manners is arrived at easily when we consider how well-mannered children typically are who learn manners at home.

Disinclination Toward Discipline

No discipline is pleasant at the time.

As a father, I can assure you that neither I nor my children enjoy the process by which I correct their bad behavior or folly. Rather, discipline is typically tedious, repetitive, and taxing.

But when we do enjoy the process of discipline, it is because we have reframed the situation from one in which we are looking only at the cost to one in which we are remembering the benefit.

Consider Hebrews 12:7-11.

> *"It is for discipline that you have to endure. God is treating you as sons. For what son is there whom his father does not discipline?*
>
> *If you are left without discipline, in which all have participated, then you are illegitimate children and not sons.*

Besides this, we have had earthly fathers who disciplined us and we respected them. Shall we not much more be subject to the Father of spirits and live? For they disciplined us for a short time as it seemed best to them, but he disciplines us for our good, that we may share his holiness.

For the moment, all discipline seems painful rather than pleasant, but later it yields the peaceful fruit of righteousness to those who have been trained by it."

Here the Christian is to understand God's relationship with us in light of the relationship we had with our fathers when they corrected our bad behaviors and attitudes. Reverse engineer the concept, though.

Here we have an affirmation in the Scriptures of the role parents in general, and fathers in particular, are supposed to play in disciplining their children.

As the text says, "all discipline seems painful rather than pleasant" in the moment. Yet we are encouraged to keep in mind the effect which discipline is intended to produce.

Discipline should not be neglected, but neither should it be conducted in a random, haphazard way.

The goal is "the peaceful fruit of righteousness" on the other end of successful discipline. And keeping our sights fixed on that fruit will help us to endure – whether we are the ones being disciplined or the ones administering discipline.

Consider this also: disciplining our children appropriately and consistently helps them understand rightly the discipline God the Father gives us.

When I first mentioned disciplining children in this chapter, some of your minds immediately turned to abusive parents. You recalled in vivid detail some harsh word from your mother. You remembered an angry and violent action from your father. You felt again the tears shed in your childhood at an unnecessary lashing out and overreaction from your parents at a relatively innocuous action or word which you had not expected would provoke the reaction they had.

But that is not what is meant by discipline here.

We do well to remember that it is neither necessary nor helpful to throw babies out with bathwater. The fact is that some undisciplined and unloving parents hurt their children and call it discipline and love. But that does not mean we should never do or say anything our children might call unpleasant when we are correcting them.

As with so many things, the existence of counterfeits does not prove the non-existence of the genuine article. A task poorly executed or committed under false pretenses does not mean the task cannot be done well or from pure motives. On the contrary, the real deal is needed all the more when imposters abound.

To overcome, we have to meditate on the fixed standard. And for the Christian in particular, that means looking to God's Word to define how, when, where, why, and to what end we as parents discipline our children.

Look to The End

Among the chief reasons my wife and I homeschool our children is to develop good character in them.

Admitting that, however, I must confess that homeschooling provides Lauren and I with ample opportunity to develop good character in ourselves also.

The fact that our children do sometimes frustrate and aggravate us by being inconsiderate, rude, undisciplined, or disobedient – that may, depending on the situation, say as much about our need to develop patience and humility as it says anything about our children needing to not unduly try our patience or embarrass us.

We have often realized in over thirteen years of parenting that sometimes our children are misbehaving or being inconsiderate because their parents were misbehaving and being inconsiderate first.

Were our children interrupting our conversation or instruction?

It took a while of my wife and I throwing our hands up in despair before it occurred to us that we ourselves are guilty of the same thing we were telling our children to not do.

Telling them "Do as I say, not as I do" is sometimes unavoidable. For instance, when our 5-year-old son asks if he can drive us all to the grocery store to buy ice cream, we do not just hand the car keys over.

All the same, our children learn best from both hearing our instruction and seeing our example lived out as we do the very same things we are telling them to do, and as we do not do the things we are telling them to not do. If we can have them do both as we say and as we do, it is all the better and less confusing.

In this way, day in and day out instruction of our children can and often does afford us an ever-present mirror for what sort of personal example we are setting. And when the example we are setting is at odds with the directions we give, homeschooling provides ample opportunity for my wife and I as mother and father to discipline ourselves.

Again, discipline is never pleasant at the time. Self-discipline is no exception.

Forgoing our self-indulgence, delaying our own gratification, putting the needs of others ahead of our own desires – these are difficult and uncomfortable. But as with our children, so also with us – we must look to the end and imagine what harvest we will reap if we sow those seeds.

To say our children are undisciplined and disobedient and obnoxious and then do nothing about it will not give us a clear conscience in the end. But if we see that they need their mother and father training them up in the way they should go, and if we apply ourselves to that end, by God's grace we will someday look back with satisfaction that we did the right thing.

God has given us this responsibility to raise our children in the fear and admonition of the Lord.

Similarly, once we realize that our reasons for not wanting to do this say a great deal about our own lack of discipline, dedication, and obedience to God, how will we have peace with God, our spouse, our children, or ourselves if we turn a blind eye and deaf ear to that reality? How can we ever be satisfied with that?

The simple answer is that we may numb ourselves to these realizations for a time. And we may self-medicate rather than self-disciplining with every distraction we can find and afford. But the better way for all parties concerned is found in our embracing rather than resisting what God has ordained in this regard, both in disciplining our children and ourselves.

By God's grace, then, we strive to keep the end goal in mind which godly discipline will produce.

And this is why we homeschool.

Chapter 13

Easier Than It Looks

Homeschooling is easier than it looks. But does it have to be easy in order to be worth it? The short answer is 'No.' But let us not take the easy way out in saying only that and no more.

If you are reading this book, you fall into one of at least two categories. You are either someone who has decided to homeschool your children, or you are not. If there is a third category, I cannot imagine what it might be, so we will stick with just the two for now.

Supposing you are someone who has decided to homeschool your children, you are either committed to it and looking for help here in explaining to other people the decision you have made, or else you are someone who is wavering in your commitment and looking for encouragement to press on.

If you are in either of these circumstances or states of mind, you already know how difficult homeschooling can be. You do not need me telling you what you already know. All the same, you do need encouragement from someone like-minded telling you to press on in pursuit of the prize at the end of this race. And this holds true whether you are still firmly resolute or faltering.

But I want to focus the time we have in this chapter on talking to the readers who belong to the second of the two chief categories I just mentioned.

Listen up, you who have not yet decided to homeschool. And everyone else who is already homeschooling will benefit just the same, and maybe even more, from putting themselves once again in the shoes of the moms and dads who have children they have yet to make up their minds about how to educate.

I will say it again, then. Homeschooling is easier than it looks. But it does not have to be easy in order to be worth it. Also, let us not kid ourselves that homeschooling is easy just because it is easier than it might seem at first glance.

Cleaning Your Room Is Hard

Homeschooling being easier than it looks does not mean that it is easy. But we should not overinflate challenges beyond reality. Such is a classic way of talking ourselves out of tackling them.

As I write this, my 7-year-old daughter Evelyn is cleaning her room and providing me with the perfect illustration of this.

Cleaning your room, according to my sources, is hard. No, it is very hard.

In my mind, cleaning my daughter Evelyn's room is easy. But then I have the benefit of years of experience. And cleaning Evelyn's room seems easy to me where it seems hard to her because I look at the task differently than she does. She sees one big mess that is going to take – and this is a direct quote – "forever."

But I see at least three or four categories of tasks which I would focus on one at a time.

Step one may be picking up all the dirty clothes and putting them in a hamper. Then she can take the hamper downstairs to the laundry room.

Step two may be picking up any miscellaneous trash scattered around the room, particularly in the center of the room where we are going to need to do most of our standing and walking and maneuvering. Then the trash can in her bedroom can be taken down and emptied into the kitchen trash can.

Step three may be picking up all the toys and putting them back in their totes and other sundry containers. Or it may be tossing the stuffed animals up onto the top bunk of her bed.

Step four may be stacking all the books and putting them back on the shelf in another room.

The point is not really what order these things are done. And these may not all be relevant or significant categories in one or another particular instance of room-cleaning.

The important lesson here is that the seemingly arduous and insurmountable task does indeed seem hard to my 7-year-old daughter because she looks at it as one big job. But it quickly becomes manageable when one big task is broken down into several smaller parts.

The same holds true of homeschooling.

One Child at A Time, One Year at A Time

If you ask my wife Lauren how difficult homeschooling all our children is now compared with when she started our oldest son Josiah in kindergarten, she will doubtless tell you it is more difficult in some ways, and much less difficult in other ways.

When Lauren first started homeschooling our children, it was as intimidating and daunting a prospect as our daughter Evelyn cleaning her room is now. Over time, however, Lauren found that breaking down the larger task of teaching each child into smaller, more manageable categories and components made the whole process more easily digestible.

Initially, Lauren was taking the long view with regards to the stakes. She did not want to ruin our oldest son Josiah. She was afraid she would fail to prepare him for a successful, healthy, happy adulthood.

What if he did not learn to read, write, or do his arithmetic?

What if he failed to develop good social skills?

All of those ways of looking to the end terrified her. Lauren was psyching herself out.

Yet once she had begun that first year and enjoyed the first signs of success, the successes increased her confidence. With more confidence, she began thinking not so much about her worst nightmares as a mother. And increasingly instead she felt free to ponder the best-case scenarios, and she let herself imagine just how good this might end up being for him and all of us.

When in the following year Lauren started teaching our second oldest son Eli as well, she was much better prepared. She had seen some of what worked and what had not worked so well. And because Eli had been listening in as Josiah went ahead of him the previous school year, Eli was already introduced to all the subjects ahead of time.

That is to say, homeschooling was never easy, *per se.* Yet it was far easier than the insurmountable, intimidating, impossible thing which had built itself up at first in my wife's imagination. And breaking the larger goal down into smaller tasks made the whole endeavor more manageable.

Cost-Benefit Analysis

One of the themes I intentionally keep coming back to in this book is the notion that we homeschool to teach our children more than just the academic subjects. Yes, those are important. And, yes, homeschooled children typically perform exceptionally well academically. Statistically and on average, they are ready for college at a consistently higher rate than their public-schooled peers. And that is good. It is great, even.

But still greater than academic excellence, we want our children to develop good character. We want them to become virtuous and noble. We want them to not only learn right from wrong in an intellectual way – as though knowing counts for anything in and of itself. Our children must be able to do what is right as well.

In their effort to both know and do what is right, or to choose what is wise rather than what is foolish, I will repeat myself in saying that instilling this capacity in our children is far easier when they have our example to follow rather than just our word to take for it.

In the spirit of that sentiment, it is worth considering how doing good but difficult things builds character.

James the brother of Jesus tells us in the New Testament book that bears his name that when we let perseverance or steadfastness have its full effect, it perfects and completes us.

As James writes in the first chapter of his letter:

"Count it all joy, my brothers, when you meet trials of various kinds, for you know that the testing of your faith produces steadfastness. And let steadfastness have its full effect, that you may be perfect and complete, lacking in nothing."

Homeschooling your child will involve trials of various kinds. It will test your faith. But that is only all the more rather than less reason to do it, particularly if it is the right thing to do. Not only will it be good for your soul. It will help your child immeasurably to see you striving to be a person of good character and conviction. So do not shy away from the challenge.

Life would be much easier in some ways if my wife and I did not homeschool. We would not be swimming upstream all the time. Our culture sends most children to be educated in the public schools. That is what most people are used to. It follows then that we homeschoolers are a foreign concept.

Cue the old Western movie trope: "You aren't from around these parts, are you?"

We hear that.

But then I take one look at the news. I consider the trends and statistics.

Most of society seems deeply confused. Men, women, and children are listless, depressed, agitated, and adrift. And when I am reminded of all of this, I can only conclude once more that going with the flow is not all it is cracked up to be. If that is where the flow is headed, we will stick with swimming upstream, thank you.

If normal is being picked on and bullied for curiosity, imagination, enthusiasm, and good manners, maybe we need a better goal than normalcy. Or perhaps we should strive for a new normal.

We need a new "new normal."

I do not hold my breath waiting for some radical sea change in which everyone is asking us to tell them how it is going to be from now on. But we have to start somewhere. And if we are going to start anywhere, the place we are best positioned to start is with ourselves and our children.

Stop thinking about what is easy. Easy in the short-term often produces hard times in the end.

We already see this in our day. But the stakes go up the longer everyone is content with bandwagons. Break away from groupthink and the herd mentality and dare to be different.

God gave us each a mind for a reason. He gave us the ability to reason for a purpose. And if we have children he purposed for us to be parents so we could lead and teach and love our children for the future.

Easy Is as Easy Does

As one final thought where ease is concerned, I want you to ask yourself a question.

Does homeschooling seem difficult in and of itself, or because of the sacrifices involved in making this choice?

If a husband and wife both work full-time and their child attends public school, homeschooling in and of itself will be challenging. But the hard thing may not be homeschooling so much as rearranging the family budget and schedule and dynamic to the point that one or the other spouse can either work from home, scale back to part-time hours, or quit their job entirely. What may be hard may not at all be homeschooling in that case so much as forgoing the second revenue stream.

And if a great many friendships and family relationships are built around public-school functions, but you suddenly decide to homeschool, the homeschooling itself may not be the hard thing. Reimagining your relationships with the people you knew – that will be.

All the same, if it provides your child with a healthier, fuller, more robust education – in character as well as academics – I believe it is worth it.

What is the extra income worth? Of what lasting value is the prestige? We are dealing with the inestimable privilege of caring for and raising eternal beings created in the image of Almighty God here.

And this is why we homeschool.

Section IV

Opposition

Chapter 14

One Big Happy Family

Let us suppose you have now decided to homeschool. Or at least let us suppose you are on board with everything thus far. Let us review what we have covered.

In the first section, we dispelled the notion that it takes a village to raise a child. We confronted the unconscious assumption that our children rightfully belong to the State before they belong to their parents. And in short, we laid the responsibility for childhood education squarely at the feet of mothers and fathers, whether or not mothers and fathers choose to homeschool their children.

In the second section, we took a long, hard look at the public education system in America. This is where most of our nation's children have received their K-12 instruction for the past century, and so it serves as the chief alternative to home education.

We considered the proposition that the origin story for humanity and the universe which is taught public schools means that survival of the fittest as an ethos pervades the way the success of children is treated in public education.

We also examined whether public schools are a conducive environment for children to learn and grow into healthy, well-adjusted adults.

Finally, we left off talking about the philosophical and historical origins of the American public education system, and we traced the roots of our present system through the legacies of Plato, Frederick the Great, and John Dewey.

In the third section, we set aside criticism of public education to look at arguments in favor of homeschooling.

We confronted the insecurity many American parents feel about teaching their own children to read, write, do arithmetic, et cetera.

We talked about the freedom inherent to homeschooling.

We also concluded that homeschooling is what we make it. I extolled the virtues of promoting virtue in your children by homeschooling – both by the nature of the instruction you give your children, and by the example you set for your children when you resolve to do challenging things like homeschooling rather than shying away from the difficulty.

Now we come to this fourth and final section, and I want to confront outside opposition to homeschooling.

Particularly if you were tracking in the first three sections, you may be thinking to yourself that all of this is well and good.

You agree that parents have the primary responsibility for their children's education.

You agree that there are a great many concerning aspects to public education.

What is more, you find the arguments for homeschooling compelling.

Your mind is almost made up. But then you hit a number of snags.

What will the response be from other people if you do this? You and your spouse may agree this is what is best for your children. But what will your extended family on both sides have to say about it?

What will your church think?

How will the laws and governing authorities of your nation, state, and locality either help or hinder you?

And finally, what about the nagging questions you still have in the back of your own mind?

In these last few chapters, we will examine opposition to your homeschooling.

Family First

What will your parents think? You might be surprised.

Mom and dad may have sent you to public school when you were a kid. But those were different times, as has already been admitted. And who can recognize that fact better than your parents?

You should ask them. How do they think the public schools have changed in the decades since they decided to send you to school?

And, by way of follow-up, would they make the same decision today? Would they still send you to public school now if they were confronted with the decision you are now facing, with the schools as they now are?

It is hard to deny that the social engineering has kicked into overdrive in recent years. And it is easy to see it has taken on a decidedly different moral bend than in decades past.

Look at teen suicide rates. Look at graduation rates and test scores. Consider readiness for college. Consider bullying and school shootings.

If your local public school had featured metal detectors and drug sniffing canines back in the day, and if so many resources for homeschooling had existed then as do now, perhaps your parents would have homeschooled you too.

Or perhaps not.

Either way, whether with good reason or not, you may be worrying that your parents would take it as a slap in the face if you chose to homeschool your children instead of sending them to the same education system dear old mom and dad sent you to.

Yet it is worth remembering how often sensibilities change when parents become grandparents. Sometimes the passing years cement convictions and opinions held from the beginning.

Other times, the wisdom that comes with experience and the perspective that comes with observing consequences over time successfully challenges the original presuppositions and stances.

My wife Lauren attended public schools all the way. But my father-in-law tells her regularly how proud he is of the two of us for homeschooling our children. If he had the choice to do it over again, would my wife and her brothers and sister have been taught at home? Maybe so, or maybe not. But my father-in-law heartily supports the decision we have made for our family all the same.

Perhaps your parents also will support your decision to homeschool more than you might expect.

As I mentioned earlier, the same was true of my Grandma Ranew before she passed. Despite a long, successful career as a public-school teacher herself in Milton, Florida, she told me over and over in recent years just how proud she was of my cousins and my family who were homeschooling.

Having seen the public schools up close from the vantage point of a dedicated educator within them for three decades, Grandma Ranew nevertheless was convinced that public schools had changed for the worse, and that it would be irresponsible and dangerous for her great-grandchildren to be educated in those same schools, given what they had become.

All in The Family

To be clear, I have not known what it is to have a hostile extended family where homeschooling is concerned.

My wife and I have always enjoyed a supportive response from our parents, grandparents, aunts, and uncles.

And if some of my aunts and uncles and cousins have chosen to send their children to public schools instead of homeschooling, I at least have never heard them criticize our choice for its contrast.

Now I realize that is more than can be said for some families, and that ours may be the exception rather than the rule in this regard. Yet I do have experience with making different choices and departing from the traditions and norms of my family in other things. And from that experience, I know that sometimes it is necessary to buck the trend. And when it is necessary, I do not believe we ought to bury our differences or avoid doing what we believe is best for our immediate family just to keep the peace in our extended family.

Yes, we ought to love and respect our extended families. God commands us to honor our father and mother, and I do not believe the relevance of that command ceases entirely just because we grow up and become adults with spouses and children of our own.

What precisely honoring our father and mother may fairly entail must change when we grow up and start our own families, though.

"For this reason, a man will leave his father and mother and cleave to his wife."

This is what the Scriptures tell us about the sacred union of marriage. And what is meant by this is that our loyalties to our family of origin must necessarily shift and give way to some extent when we take a spouse. When we get married, is it no longer appropriate for us to be loyal first to our parents. Rather, after we recite our vows 'til death do us part, our primary human relationship becomes that which we enjoy with our spouse. And once children enter the fray, our next responsibility after our spouse within our immediate family is to our children.

If you and your significant other have talked about all this homeschooling business and the most significant objection to crossing the Rubicon is that your parents may not approve, a few observations are worth noting.

First, any parent and grandparent who thinks foremost of taking personal offense at your decision to homeschool your child because that is not how they chose to have you educated is suffering a lapse into self-absorption. They are not loving their son or daughter, son-in-law or daughter-in-law, or grandson and granddaughter as well as they might.

We can hope this is a passing madness and they will take themselves in hand shortly.

Suppose they do not take themselves in hand. If that is the way they stubbornly are, you should not be leading and loving your immediate family – either your spouse or your children – based off the selfish insecurities of your parents.

Moreover, if the selfishness of your parent is the chief obstacle to you homeschooling your child, perhaps this indicates all the more that you need to do this thing as a way of recalibrating the dynamic in your family – both immediate and extended – to something healthier and more reasonable.

If the reasons for homeschooling are good – both from the standpoint of practical wisdom and principled righteousness – then failing to do the good thing does not suddenly become nobler just because a tenuous argument could be made about honoring your father and mother who do not want you to do that objectively good thing.

Consider what Jesus says in Luke 14:26.

> *"If anyone comes to me and does not hate his own father and mother and wife and children and brothers and sisters, yes, and even his own life, he cannot be my disciple."*

The diligent student of God's Word knows Jesus here is not making an absolute statement. We are commanded elsewhere to love and honor all of these people Jesus is referring to.

What Jesus is getting at is the order of operations. We must love God first and best, and our first loyalty is to him.

But if our relationship with any other person – even our parents, siblings, spouse, or children – puts us in an awkward spot where we are told we cannot obey and honor what God has commanded of us, then we choose God. And if anyone else has a problem with that, they will just have to get over themselves.

Just so, if God has put it in your heart to homeschool your children, but your extended family disapproves and wants to take personal offense at that or put your relationship with them in jeopardy over the decision as a kind of hostage-taking, then do the right thing anyway. All the more if you have arrived at this conviction after diligent prayer and studying of God's Word.

Settling Conflicts of Interest

In a perfect world, such ideas as honoring your father and mother would never come into conflict with doing the right thing by your spouse and children.

But then we do well to remember that this is not a perfect world.

This world is tainted by the curse of sin. And we are a fallen race often marred in our faculties by the effects of a sinful nature – both in ourselves and those around us.

Therefore, we must have reliable tiebreakers when righteousness and doing the honorable thing seem to indicate two mutually exclusive courses of action.

In the marriage relationship, the New Testament tells us that wives are to submit to their husbands in everything, and that husbands likewise are to love their wives in the same way Christ loved the Church, laying his life down for her.

Yet none of this talk of submission and self-sacrifice works the way it is supposed to outside the broader context of both the husband and wife submitting themselves to God in Christ Jesus and striving to trust and obey what has been delivered to us in the Bible.

When ranking the importance of our relationships, the place of chief importance must belong to God.

Jesus answers in Matthew 22: 34-40 when asked by a lawyer which is the greatest commandment in the Law.

"You shall love the Lord your God with all your heart and with all your soul and with all your mind. This is the great and first commandment. And a second is like it: You shall love your neighbor as yourself. On these two commandments depend all the Law and the Prophets."

As Jesus answers this, our absolute love for God is primary. Our love for our neighbor is secondary.

Though our love for our fellow man is intimately related to our love for God, and ultimately flows from it like a tributary stream branching off of a larger river. It cannot be confused as the guiding source.

As an aside, I find what Jesus tells both the lawyer and us here to be very interesting. These two commandments summarize all the Law and the Prophets – that is to say, they sum up the Old Testament.

But return again to the question at hand.

What are we supposed to do when an apparent conflict arises between the command to love God with every aspect of our being on the one hand, and the command to love our neighbor as we love ourselves on the other?

The short answer is that we must obey God rather than men. Our love for God not only supersedes our love for our neighbor. Our love for God informs our love for our fellow man, and what all can or cannot be entailed by it.

So also with apparent conflicts between loving and honoring our immediate family well and abiding by the wishes and inclinations of our extended family.

Chapter 15

Moving on from family matters, we come to what for some is a thornier source of external opposition. Consider the role our local church might play in our decision of whether and how to homeschool our children. This is a big enough topic that I will cover it in this chapter and the next.

First off, let me start out by confessing that one of the most disheartening things I have realized over the years is just how unfriendly some churches are to homeschooling.

Since homeschooling is not just an abstract idea, but is a way of life for actual families, those churches which are unfriendly to the idea of homeschooling often turn out to be unfriendly to the families which embrace this way of life.

I say this from painful experience.

Now I am thankful to report that our experience has improved dramatically in this regard over the years. Whether this is due to evolving sensibilities in the culture around us, or whether we have gotten better at choosing churches which are friendlier to homeschooling, or whether God has supernaturally intervened to lead us to an oasis in the desert – I cannot tell which is the case.

So I choose to believe that all of the above is the case in some measure, with extra weight and credit given to God's provision.

When I was a kid, homeschooling was still a novel concept. In the 1990's, some churches would flat-out tell homeschooling mothers and fathers that they were sinning to pull their children out of public schools to teach them at home.

This is actually happened to one of my aunts. When she chose to homeschool my cousins, a visit was paid her by a few of the ladies from their church local.

A good, godly woman otherwise, my aunt was nevertheless informed in no uncertain terms that what she was doing was wrong. And she was subsequently called to repent in short order.

In my own personal experience as a homeschooled kid from kindergarten through 11th grade, I remember my awareness of this dynamic growing clearer as I got older.

When in high school my dad and brother and I attended First Baptist Church of Hillsboro, Ohio, one of the public-school teachers who had attended there for a long old time actually had the audacity to tell me at a certain point that I was not like other homeschoolers. I was well-spoken and intelligent. And I remember him saying this in a smug, disaffected, unimpressed sort of way.

I received as much of a back-handed compliment as the man at church was prepared to give me before turning to go talk with someone else more comfortable to his sensibilities and prejudices.

The context of that conversation, by the way, was that he and I had been discussing how I had tried out for the lead role in the Hillsboro High School rendition of The Music Man.

A number of anonymous persons in the community had complained to the school after I was given a small supporting role in the barbershop quartet.

When the next theater production was announced, I was planning to audition again, but was told that homeschoolers were not allowed to participate anymore.

That off-putting conversation with the public-school teacher at our church was the closest thing to an explanation I ever got.

I was not like most homeschoolers. In other words, the snide dismissal of my trying out was that most homeschoolers had a reputation in the public school system for being something other than well-spoken, well-mannered, and capably intelligent.

Fast-forwarding several years. When my wife Lauren and I had our own children and were attending Good News Gathering – another church in the same town – I will never forget the pastor addressing a question someone had asked privately as to whether that church would ever consider starting its own private Christian school.

Emphatically not, announced the pastor from the pulpit. Their mission was to send their children into the public schools as missionaries. Starting their own private Christian school would be antithetical to that.

On the drive home from church that Sunday, I asked my wife what that implied about the way this church in general, but particularly the leadership of the church perceived our decision to homeschool.

If pulling children out of the public schools was seen as somehow less spiritual by virtue of the analogy that our children should be missionaries in the public schools, how much more-so did they look with disdain at our children not even being missionaries in a private Christian school?

Little Missionaries

In my experience, this has always been the line of attack on homeschooling from within the church, especially by pastors. The children from Christian homes should be sent to public schools so their testimony can serve as salt and light in an otherwise godless education system.

Yet this argument has always befuddled me. It seems rather nakedly superficial, and not terribly compelling when you really think about it.

Suppose my wife Lauren and I were to announce tomorrow we were moving to China to serve as missionaries there. And suppose we went around to churches and missionary organizations asking for their logistical and financial support. We would be bombarded with a whole lot of very pointed, specific, and practical questions.

How long have we been Christians?

How sound is our doctrine?

Are we mature in our own faith sufficient to not only share the gospel with those who do not know Christ, but also to resist the influence of a godless foreign culture which neither knows Jesus nor recognizes him as Lord and Savior when it hears about him?

And besides these spiritual considerations, I know for a fact that we would in many quarters be required to have a bachelor's degree at least before any missions organization would associate itself with our effort.

Besides that, we would need some plan for supporting ourselves financially.

If not wholly depending on churches and missionary organizations for donations, my wife and I would need some kind of profitable vocation to pursue in that foreign land in order to give us independent standing and a means for interacting with the local public in a dignified, respectable way.

Moreover, in the case of a foreign country where some other language besides English was the primary language, we would need to acquire fluency in order to be effective.

And besides learning the language, we would have to learn the history and culture of that people to whom we were intending to bring the gospel.

But all of this preparatory work would only be encouraged if we had first satisfied our inquisitors as to the first questions of our spiritual maturity, education level, and practical means. And the task of checking all those boxes would likely take many months if not years of preparation before we were finally sent off with the thoughts and prayers of our local churches in tow.

Yet no such organized effort at preparing our children for supposed missionary work in the public schools is ever so much as hinted at, much less proffered by those who insist our children from Christian homes must attend the public schools to be missionaries in them. This, to my mind, makes the argument patently absurd on its face.

The naked truth is that children from Christian homes are not naturally prepared to be missionaries to anyone, much less an aggressively atheistic educational system which more often strips Christian faith from its charges rather than being converted by them.

Moreover, there is no evidence whatsoever to suggest it is either righteous or responsible for us to expect supernatural preparation in this case. Nor should we suppose that children with Christian parents acquire by osmosis the ability to both live out their faith and propagate it in a hostile environment merely by virtue of having Christian parents.

Yet if we will suppose and assume such things regardless, without any evidence that they are sound, I fully expect in the name of consistency that the obstacle course which adult missionaries must run in order to be missionaries to foreign nations like China should be treated similarly henceforth.

In the interest of consistency, let us all hold our collective breath for churches and missions organizations to cut blank checks to any adult who stands up in their midst saying they want to be missionaries to foreign lands.

Let us send the whole lot off smartly with as little preparation and diligence as is given to our children who are sent to American public schools to serve as little missionaries there.

You can guess about as well as I can how likely that is to prove successful.

Pray About It

While we are on the subject of missionaries, another experience comes to mind from when we attended Good News Gathering in Hillsboro, Ohio.

I remember the response I got when I approached Brad, the associate pastor about a decade ago expressing interest in joining an upcoming mission trip.

Every year, Good News Gathering would send a team of adults and teenagers to Haiti to help with work projects at the La Croix Mission.

After one such trip and a visit from Pastor Pierre – our partner in Haiti – Jeff, the head pastor of Good News Gathering, announced to the congregation that there were funds available for anyone in our local church who wanted to join the team the next year. If anyone were interested in going, but could not personally afford the trip, they ought to talk with the pastors of GNG about it, and perhaps something could be worked out to facilitate.

This I did. Approaching Brad, I referenced what Jeff had said in the recent sermon, and I offered myself up as another pair of hands and feet for the Lord's work in Haiti.

What was the response I received? Brad encouraged me to "Pray about it."

That was a very Christian response. And we read in the Scriptures that we should pray without ceasing. So I cannot legitimately object to the counsel I received.

All the same, given the brevity of Brad's response, and the apparent lack of follow-up questions or encouragement to come back after praying about it, and the total lack of acknowledgement that I may have already prayed about it – all of these together communicated to me that what our associate pastor actually meant was that he did not think this was a good idea, and he wanted me to drop it.

And so I did. I promptly gave up on the idea, having my answer near enough in the admonition. Perhaps the funds were meant for someone else. Or perhaps there were not so many funds as had been implied by the lead pastor. Or perhaps Jeff and Brad did not think I was adequately well-formed to be of much help on this particular mission.

In any event, it was just as well. The Lord's will was not that I should go to Haiti. So I did not go.

But now that response which Brad gave to me those many years ago rings in my ears. And that same response is what I would say to the pastors who blithely tell their congregants that they should send their children bravely into the public schools to serve as little missionaries.

Pray about it.

Chapter 16

A Tale of Two Churches

Your local church can serve as either an encouragement or an impediment to the homeschooling family. We have experienced both situations up-close and personally.

Before moving from Eastern Montana to Northeastern Colorado in September of 2019, my wife and I attended Christian and Missionary Alliance churches. When we lived in Glendive – my hometown – we attended Glendive Alliance. And when we moved to Sidney, we eventually settled on attending the CMA church about 15 miles to the south in Savage for about four-and-a-half years.

During our attendance at that little CMA church in Savage, Montana, I was asked to serve in leadership. Initially asked to serve as an elder, I consented. Then when I was asked to serve as a deacon, I did that instead. And for several years, I was puzzled by the question of why I was initially asked to serve as an elder only to have the offer changed to deacon after being put to the governing board.

Never before in my professional life have I received and accepted a job offer only to have my prospective employer demote me before my official start date. I have declined initial job offers before only to be offered more money and better benefits from the prospective employer as an effort on their part to sweeten the pot. But this experience at the little church in Eastern Montana was a novel one, and a head-scratcher for quite some time.

The years passed, however. And after a great deal of my repeatedly asking the persons involved, I eventually was given an answer.

As it turned out, a certain influential and established family in the church and community had raised concerns about another elder being added to the governing board who did not have his own children in the local public school, and who was not himself either teaching or coaching in that same local school.

"Wouldn't it be nice if our whole governing board was involved in the local school?"

That was the question one of the relatives of the elder who finally answered my inquiries eventually told me he had been asked when my candidacy for elder was announced to their family on the governing board.

And so, for the sake of optics in the community, and because that same influential family was sending all their children to the public school, and because several of the men and women in that family were teachers and coaches in the same local public school, my appointment to leadership in the church was whittled down before it had begun.

I eventually learned what had happened, but not until years of service had passed. Between my family homeschooling, and my blogging and social media posts critical of the public education system, I had offended this leading family in the church and community.

They were not content for the offense pass, nor did they want to reward me with increased standing and authority within their church or community. Whatever my other qualifications for the position, the fact that I had challenged the status quo and their vanity disqualified me for lasting or significant service there.

This sentiment in time ultimately led to my resigning my post at the end of my first 2-year term as deacon. And it was not but 8-months later that the good Lord led us to move our family out of Montana and to Colorado.

Truth, Beauty, and Goodness

By contrast, I cannot adequately describe the experience we enjoyed shortly after moving to Colorado with anything short of Providential.

Within the first few weeks of moving into our rental home in Greeley, my wife met our neighbors two houses down. Like us, JP and Monica Chavez had recently moved to the neighborhood. And they had three young children – a daughter about our daughter Evelyn's age, and twin boys about the ages of our second-to-youngest son Enoch.

On the way to pick up the mail from the mailbox, my wife Lauren had to call our children out of the Chavez's front yard.

Only after Lauren had called our children back did she realize that their children were also there. Why were they not in school? Perhaps they were another homeschooling family like us.

Sure enough.

A conversation struck up between Lauren and Monica, and shortly thereafter I got a text message at work. Monica had invited Lauren to the ladies' small group that evening at her house. I encouraged Lauren to go. And when she came home and told me how kind and welcoming all the ladies there at small group had been, she also told me they had invited our family to visit their church that coming Sunday.

And so, within a short time of our arriving in Greeley, the first church we attended was Summitview Community Church in Evans, Colorado.

Based out of a former furniture store by the railroad tracks, everyone here too was very kind and welcoming.

And to my enduring surprise and delight, when the man who had been leading praise and worship came up to shake my hand and introduce himself after the service was over, he asked me how many children we had.

"We have seven," I said.

He grinned widely and answered.

"Oh, nice! We have eight."

On the 15-minute drive home from church that afternoon, my wife and children and I excitedly compared notes.

There were so many children in the church – probably as many or more children as adults.

And between the women my wife had talked with and the men I had talked with, it quickly became clear that large homeschooling families were welcome, though by no means required, at this church.

In the following weeks and months of attending, we were delighted to find out that not only were we no longer so conspicuous for having what these days is considered a large family – several other families in the church were about our size, through combinations of natural-born children and adopted children.

We were also no longer conspicuous for homeschooling our large family, since about half the families in the church also homeschooled.

And not only were we not the only large homeschooling family. There were several other families in the church who used the same curriculum we use.

And not only were there several other large homeschooling families in the church who used the same curriculum we did. Those families even had a homeschooling group that met at the church each Wednesday afternoon to do supplemental activities like art, poetry, and public speaking, and to help and encourage one another in figuring out how to teach their children at home.

The sweet serendipity of it was thrilling, and we are still astounded by the Lord's goodness a year in to attending this church, joining small groups, sending our children to the youth group, and joining that aforementioned homeschool group.

In fact, this church situation we believe so Providential is the first instance in my life which has provoked me to even think of using the word serendipity as I search for words to describe the wonder of it.

Stark Contrast

The contrast in church experiences between these two could hardly be starker. And it just goes to show what a difference your local church can make.

Your local church can serve as either an encouragement or an impediment to homeschooling, and we have experienced both situations up-close and personally to be able to attest to that.

In the one case, we eventually came to dread attending church. Every meeting was tense and off-putting in some way. The people who were offended by my criticism of public education were standoffish.

After four and a half years of attending, and even taking up a leadership role in the church – keeping the grounds, cleaning the church, teaching Sunday school for high schoolers and adults, leading worship, and even filling the pulpit, we felt more and more like outsiders and foreigners the longer we were there.

This made us feel lonely, isolated, besieged, and rejected. It discouraged and distracted us from the task we felt strongly convicted to undertake as a family. And I personally lost a lot of sleep in those years, trying to puzzle out a peaceable way to resolve the conflict.

In the other case, we now look forward with relish to meeting together.

To be clear, we do not all always agree with our newfound church family. But then that is to be expected anywhere people with independent minds and individual callings assemble for any purpose or length of time.

There is far more that unites us than divides us.

And not only do we find encouragement in the abstract in this church. We find in joining others who are likeminded and supportive – who are themselves engaged in the same audacious pursuit we are – that many practical benefits come when the local church body is able to give advice as to how to go about overcoming the real challenges which come with having a large homeschooling family as we do.

There is more than compassion there. There is a kind of empathy which can only occur when shared experiences cause others to know your joys and sorrows on a personal level as you know them.

Moreover, when those others may even be a few years farther down the road you are traveling, they can give you helpful advice which comes from having both made and corrected the same mistakes you have made, are making, and will make in the future.

This really does get to the heart of what the church historically has been about, and what the Scriptures tell us is the purpose of the church.

Now I hope you do not hear what I am not saying here. I am not saying that the core mission of the church is to encourage everyone to have large homeschooling families. The core purpose of the church is to honor and worship God, to teach and study the Word, and to make disciples of all nations.

Yet the truth is that where Christians have families, the local church ought to be about encouraging the greatest possible diligence and fidelity in organizing our families in a way that maximizes the Great Commission, and the special calling God has placed on Christians to follow Christ.

The beautiful reality is that making disciples must, if and when we have children, begin in our own homes with those children.

As the Apostle Paul writes in the New Testament to two of his disciples – Timothy and Titus – part of what qualifies overseers and deacons is whether they manage their own homes well. This is not a reference to interior decorating and arranging furniture.

What the Apostle Paul is specifically alluding to is the way a man loves and leads his wife and children. This is of such importance that a man failing to love and lead his family well disqualifies him for an official leadership role in the church.

In other words, the home is where Christian leaders are to be not only formed, but also tested and tried. In the home and family, would-be and prospective leaders either demonstrate that they possess the requisite character to teach, nurture, and govern God's people, or else they are weighed and measured and found wanting for that line of work.

In light of this, why do we suffer so much nonsense about Christian mothers and fathers sub-contracting their children's education and upbringing so they can be freed up themselves for ministry?

*"**Children are not a distraction from more important work. They are the most important work.**"*

Whether C.S. Lewis originally said this or not, this saying is often attributed to him. And whether it is misattributed to Lewis or not, there is a truth to the statement which we as Christians do well to remember and apply to the way we organize ourselves, our homes, and our churches.

And this is why we homeschool.

Chapter 17

Friends, Romans, Countrymen

Making the best choice for your child's education may cost you socially. Your friends may take offense. They may feel you are looking down on them if you exit the public education system which they are not prepared to similarly criticize or leave.

And if your interactions with the parents of your children's classmates have revolved around school functions, your public schooling friends may not make special time to get together with you and your family if you and your children no longer have any reason to attend those school functions.

This may well be the reality of your situation. And that is unfortunate if so. All the same, friends, Romans, and countrymen, lend me your ears.

But if those friends and acquaintances in the public education system care so little as all that for spending time with you, they are perhaps not the deepest and most enduring kinds of friends and acquaintances you could hope for.

This may come as a painful realization. But the people you associate with most often – if indeed they do so primarily out of boredom and convenience – may not be such great friends anyway.

Remember also that peer pressure does not only affect children. The thought of breaking away from the herd to pursue greener pastures elsewhere is often frightening to adults too because we also are susceptible to peer pressure.

The compulsion to conform to what most people around us are doing is one of the strongest forces in psychology. And it is all the stronger for being subconscious and often overlooked.

We think without thinking that the majority of people around us are doing what they do because they have considered all the alternatives and concluded that this is the wisest, most effective, most efficient course of action.

In the absence of a better idea, it is easier to go with the flow. Follow the crowd. Let the current take you. Join the herd.

Yet safety in numbers is no safety at all when groupthink sets in and serves to reinforce dysfunctional modes of relating – both to one another and to our circumstances.

What is more, when groupthink reacts with hostility to a new idea because of its potential to disrupt our comfortable cruise control lives, the herd can quickly go from being our native ally to being outright hostile.

All too often, the herd irrationally concludes you are either with it or against it.

It has been said by people wiser than I that the surest way to get someone to change their behavior is to laugh at them. And this is proven by experience.

So, we think proactively about whether people will ridicule or mock us for choosing to homeschool our children. And that can serve as a powerful deterrent from pursuing the idea further, at least openly.

You talk in hushed tones with trusted confidants. The friend or family member you gather may be sympathetic is the one you leak the news to first to test the waters.

You are considering pulling your children out of public school and homeschooling them.

There is still a lot of research and reading to do, and you need to talk more with your husband or wife about it first.

Some details remain to work out as to how you might do it, and you still need to look into what the laws in your area actually are.

There are so many options for curriculum, and you do not yet know what it would look like for one of the two income-earners to stay home. But you are thinking seriously about it.

Too many concerning developments and stories have come to your attention for you to carry on without at least examining other options. Right?

Now the person in whom you are confiding laughs. They make it into a joke and tell you they think you would be a terrible teacher.

They point out how undisciplined you are, and how much you complain about waking up early to take your kids to school. You read so little, and you occasionally misspell things, or whatever.

If you are fainthearted, this is all it takes for you to bury your reservations once and for all.

But wait a second. Who did you confide in? And what were their reasons for scoffing?

As J.P. Morgan once famously quipped:

> *"A man always has two reasons for doing anything: a good reason and the real reason."*

So also with your family, friends, and acquaintances who might mock the idea of homeschooling. The reason they give you for scoffing may sound sensible at first blush. But have you considered whether that was their real reason?

Their real reason might be that they genuinely do not think you are up to the challenge. They might just be trying to look out for you.

Yet just as easily, they may be thinking of your potential new course first and foremost in terms of how it would adversely impact them.

Perhaps they would make time for you outside of school functions. But in all your preparation and execution of this homeschooling idea, would you make time for them?

And if you were stressed out and aggravated with homeschooling your children, would they know how to counsel you through it?

If not, perhaps they are afraid you are going down a path which they do not know how to help you be successful on. These are uncharted waters for you if you have never homeschooled before. And if your friend or family has never homeschooled either, how are they supposed to know how to assist or encourage you?

Besides these, your friend may know people who homeschooled unsuccessfully. Or perhaps they saw a negative story about a homeschooling family in the news or on social media. Now they fear for you that the same things which were said about that family – rightly or not – will be said about you and your family.

All of these and other considerations could sway your confidant in counseling you one way or the other without bad motives entering into the equation.

Good motives or ill, however, consider who it is you are confiding in – before, during, and after seeking their counsel. Make a mental note in the margins of your mind how much weight to put on the reasons they give you, and what or whether they might hold back for fear of seeming uninformed, unhelpful, or selfish.

Pursue Good Experience

My wife and I recently celebrated fourteen years of marriage. It occurred to us in looking back on our time together thus far that we have not only had seven children in fourteen years. We have also lived in three states and enjoyed all manner of adventures and misadventures.

Now as I write this it occurs to me that whenever my wife and I are considering a big move, job change, or attending a different church – any major departure from our current course in pursuit of a new possibility – we both pray asking the Lord for wisdom, and we seek out people with good experience and demonstrated good judgment in that regard.

When we first began considering marriage, we made up our minds that we wanted to have a successful marriage. And in determining that we wanted a successful marriage, we discussed who we knew whose marriage we considered successful.

Who could we talk with who would be able to tell us what they had learned through trial and error, but also ultimately from achieving a modicum of what to us looked like the sort of family dynamic we wanted to emulate?

The couple we decided to approach was Mark and Laurie Flower.

Their two biological children – a daughter named Molly and a son named Zack – were about our age. Besides these, they also had nine – yes, nine – adopted children from Haiti, who were all a fair amount younger than us, and ran the gamut as far as ages.

The Flowers also homeschooled. And they also from time to time hosted a Bible study for teens at their home in the country near Leesburg, Ohio.

I met Mark and Laurie through my part-time high school job at the Highland County YMCA. Lauren got to know them through the Bible study they hosted.

Both Lauren and I were impressed from all our interactions with the cheerful and loving way the Flowers as a family related to one another.

Their children were polite, enthusiastic, creative, energetic, intelligent, and well-spoken.

And Mark and Laurie always seemed to have a smile on their face, and a warmth in the way they related to one another, their children, and everyone else they met.

In short, to sum them up in one word, they seemed genuinely happy.

So when we asked them to sit down with us for lunch one day at the local Frisch's Big Boy diner in Hillsboro, we explained what we were asking of them in the way of advice. Then we listened with rapt attention as they explained how they had met, courted, and started their married life.

Mark and Laurie told us what they believed about how God's Word describes and proscribes marriage and parenting.

And both Mark and Laurie sincerely and enthusiastically encouraged us to pursue our intentions for one another in light of God's Word and a sober understanding that sometimes marriage and parenting is hard. But it is no less a blessing and reward for being difficult.

The advice I would give to you if you are considering homeschooling is to do likewise.

Look around. Ask around. Seek out a couple you know who has been there and done that, yes.

But more than just someone with experience, you want counsel from someone who has good experience. So talk with a couple who can counsel you in how to do this thing successfully.

Find someone to talk with who is ahead of you on this road. Get individualized counsel from people who are getting it right.

Naysayers Gonna Say Nay

All too often when people go asking for advice, they go looking for wisdom in all the wrong places. Yes, you can get knowledge from reading magazine articles with catchy headlines. And, yes, sometimes a good book on the subject yields insight. Hopefully, this book you are reading now has proven such for you.

But there is nothing quite like talking with a real flesh and blood person whose character and track record you have seen up close and in person.

As with what we discussed earlier, it is all very well and good to tell someone to do this or that thing, particularly if the thing that needs doing is correct but difficult. Yet it is quite another thing to demonstrate by actions how to do a thing correctly, and to model the kinds of behaviors and attitudes which have been prescribed.

Jesus puts it well in Luke 7:35.

"Yet wisdom is justified by all her children."

If you go looking for advice and encouragement from people who have not proven themselves successful in accomplishing the thing you have in mind to do, you may get advice and encouragement.

But how will you know whether it is good advice unless you are able to see whether the principles, when applied consistently, produce a beneficial and desirable result?

You do not just want to do the thing. You want to do it well. So leave off asking naysayers what they think unless you want to hear 'Nay.'

And if you really do mean business about homeschooling, find experienced homeschoolers who will steer you in the right direction.

Chapter 18

The Man in the Mirror

At the end of the day, the only person you really need to persuade about homeschooling is yourself and your spouse. This decision firmly resides with you as the father and mother of your children, and everyone else's opinion is incidental.

For all the hypothetical scenarios and amateurish psychoanalysis of your family, friends, and local church, what other people think is not nearly so important as we too often tell ourselves.

If homeschooling can objectively be shown to be the right thing to do before God – and we need to be Bereans about this and search the Scriptures daily to see whether these things are so – then you may indeed face opposition from every quarter. You probably will not, but so what if you do? What does that amount to?

If this is objectively the right thing to do, then do it anyway despite external opposition. Maybe you win the naysayers over in time by executing successfully.

But this one thing I can tell you for sure: you will never win the stubbornly opposed to your way of seeing things if you let their negative and mistaken opinions rule your life.

The point is really not to do or not do the right thing primarily to win people over to your side anyway.

If you do a bang-up job of homeschooling your child and the critics affirm your decision in the end, consider it an added bonus.

The ultimate prize is being a good steward of the responsibility and opportunity which God has entrusted to you as a parent.

The goal then must be to hear those sweet words of affirmation from the Savior:

"Well done, good and faithful servant. Enter now into your place of rest."

This is not to say that homeschooling will save you and your children.

As Christians, we believe that "You were saved by grace through faith, not of works lest any man should boast."

But for those of us who are already saved by the blood of the Lamb, we want the fact that we have been saved by God's grace to color every area of our personal and family lives forever after our realization of the great gift we have already been given.

This includes but is not limited to the way we train up our children after us in the way they should go.

This includes but is by no means limited to the task of making disciples by starting in our own home with our own sons and daughters.

And maybe just maybe, as we let our lights so shine before all men that they might see our good works, they will indeed glorify our Father in Heaven.

Maybe just maybe as we train up our children in the way they should go, we fit ourselves and them for Heaven just a little more every day.

And maybe just maybe if we choose to homeschool our children as part of taking every thought captive to Christ we will make disciples more than just converts.

Our children will not just pray a prayer. They will not just go to church with us once or twice a week, join the youth group, and sing in the choir, or play a shepherd or wise man in the Christmas pageant once a year.

Maybe just maybe if we really apply ourselves to the task of teaching our children to read, write, and do math in a way that consistently reveres our Creator in whose image we were made, we will deliver to our children an integrated worldview which prepares them to be salt and light in a world that desperately needs Christians who are not only reasonable and able to reason, but also open to reason.

And this is why we homeschool.

My wife Lauren and I homeschool our children in hopes that they grow from acorns up into mighty oaks of conviction, humility, and graciousness.

In humility, we recognize that Yahweh is our only God. Jesus is our only King. Our God is the God of all gods, the Lord of all lords, and the Master to whom we dedicate our lives.

And as we seek to honor our Maker, we inescapably learn to honor one another better each day.

In the strength of our convictions, we welcome gladly trials of our faith because we know that the testing of our faith develops perseverance in us of a sort which is indispensable for completing and perfecting us for the purpose God created us and placed us in our peculiar context to achieve.

By God's grace, we press on to fulfill the calling of the Lord delivered by the prophet Jeremiah.

> *"Thus says the Lord of hosts, the God of Israel, to all the exiles whom I have sent into exile from Jerusalem to Babylon: Build houses and live in them; plant gardens and eat their produce. Take wives and have sons and daughters; take wives for your sons, and give your daughters in marriage, that they may bear sons and daughters; multiply there, and do not decrease. But seek the welfare of the city where I have sent you into exile, and pray to the Lord on its behalf, for in its welfare you will find your welfare."*

By God's grace, we relate to the exiled children of Israel in Babylon who wondered why they were living in a land that often forgets the one true God and seeks not at all to honor the same except in vague references on the currency and old carvings on government buildings which have not yet caught the attention of atheists, but surely will sooner than later.

And as we strive to not be hypocrites who honor God with our lips while our hearts are far away, we thank the Lord that he gives more grace.

Yet where we see that we ought to build homes in which to reside, and that wisdom is demonstrated by filling our homes with every good thing, we pray for wisdom also to raise our sons and daughters to someday make good husbands and wives themselves.

We multiply and do not decrease.

And in all this, we seek the welfare of the cities to which God has brought us since there is apparently no conflict between finding our welfare and praying to the Lord our God that his will is done on Earth as it is in Heaven.

Then Make A Change

Consider the chorus of a famous song by the late Michael Jackson.

I am starting with the man in the mirror

I am asking him to change his ways

And no message could have been any clearer

If you wanna make the world a better place

Take a look at yourself and then make a change

Here again, do not hear what I am not saying.

We should not pattern our lives or our family dynamics off a Michael Jackson song.

His story was a tragic one which illustrates as well as any the importance of training up a child in the way he should go. His father was abusive and negligent, and the late Mr. Jackson grew up very lost, confused, and wounded as a direct result.

Yet there is a sentiment communicated in this song which bears truth we do well to consider.

It is all very well and good to recognize the many problems in the world. And I realize that criticizing the state of the church and our government here in America is very fashionable.

At a certain point, however, it behooves us to ask what actually makes a difference in any dysfunctional situation if our default mode is closed off to changing our own ways of thinking, feeling, speaking, and acting.

I will never forget when early in our marriage Lauren and I took a vacation to spend a few weeks with her Uncle Gary and Aunt Sheri's family near Omaha, Nebraska.

Their homeschooling family of seven living out in the country was a significant encouragement to us, and they taught us a great deal by their speech and conduct.

But while we were staying with Uncle Gary and Aunt Sheri's family, we visited their church. And I will never forget being part of a conversation among several of the young men in the church at the pastor's home after the service one Sunday.

Somehow or another, Michael Jackson came up in conversation. Someone mentioned him, and one among the young men – most or all of whom had been homeschooled their entire lives – blurted out that he had never heard of Michael Jackson.

"I was homeschooled," he declared proudly by way of explanation.

Having been homeschooled myself from little on up, I could not help laughing out loud.

"So was I, but I have definitely heard of Michael Jackson!"

The look on my face must have been sufficiently incredulous because the conversation promptly died at that point, and that was the end of it.

That brief exchange has stuck with me all these years. And I think the reason for this is that it seemed a kind of boasting in ignorance.

Lord forgive me. And I hope also that young man and his companions will too if they ever read this. We all have our moments, and that just happened to be one of his.

Or at least that was my opinion at the time. And it continues to be.

Michael Jackson was a deeply flawed, broken person. And even his song seems a cry for help as much as a call to action. He realized he has been self-absorbed and oblivious to the problems and suffering of others of the world.

So maybe 'Man in the Mirror' achieved some of what it was produced and distributed to.

Or maybe this was a kind of penance. Or maybe it was all about selling records and making money.

Only the good Lord knows for sure.

Yet what I know is that when Jesus told the tale of the two men praying in the temple, the one who could not even look up to heaven as he beat his breast and begged for mercy from God – that was the man who went away justified.

And the Pharisee who looked proudly up to heaven and thanked God that he was not like that sinner over there beating his chest – that man apparently needed no help at all. Or so he thought.

To be clear, I believe that the single greatest reason we should homeschool our children is to recognize and combat our own innate selfishness and sinfulness, and to make the world a better place for God's glory by starting with ourselves and our children.

As Dr. Jordan Peterson once put it, we should try making our beds and cleaning our rooms every day before we set about to criticizing the world. When we do that, we suddenly realize how difficult even just cleaning our room can be. And when we tell our children to do it, we suddenly realize how difficult the task of getting them to clean their rooms can be. Believe me. I speak from experience.

Yet I want to leave you off with more than Michael Jackson lyrics and quotes from Jordan Peterson. So consider at the last here what Jesus said.

> *"Judge not, that you be not judged. For with the judgment you pronounce you will be judged, and with the measure you use it will be measured to you. Why do you see the speck that is in your brother's eye, but do not notice the log that is in your own eye? Or how can you say to your brother, 'Let me take the speck out of your eye,' when there is the log in your own eye? You hypocrite, first take the log out of your own eye, and then you will see clearly to take the speck out of your brother's eye."*

What this passage is telling us is not that we should never point out the shortcomings of others. Nor does Jesus mean by this that "judge not" can now rightly be added as an eleventh commandment besides the famous ten which God wrote with his finger on two tablets of stone.

On the contrary, what is being described here is a way of testing whether our motives really are to love God with all our being and to love our neighbor as we love ourselves when we start criticizing wrongdoing and folly in the world around us before we have confronted it in our own homes.

If we love to find fault with everyone else yet fail to do what is in our power to do about our own sin and silliness, we are disingenuous hypocrites.

Yet genuinely loving God and one another means we start first with correcting what is correctable in us; only after we have done this do we tell others how they need to be.

As Abraham Lincoln once quipped to a man who asked him during the Civil War whether he supposed God was on the side of the Union.

"My concern is not whether God is on our side; my greatest concern is to be on God's side, for God is always right."

Mr. Lincoln was homeschooled, by the way. And the family Bible was how he learned to read at a young age.

Despite President Lincoln's mother dying when he was only 9 years old, and numerous other personal tragedies besides the United States of America breaking in half after his election to the presidency, our nation's 16th president drew from a wealth of personal strength and wisdom which was deeply and firmly implanted by the Scriptures being so central to his upbringing.

And believe it or not, this too is why we homeschool.

Made in the USA
Las Vegas, NV
12 January 2024

84259815R00146